The Double Tree

SELECTED POEMS   1942–1976

Also by Judith Wright

POEMS
The Moving Image
Woman to Man
The Gateway
The Two Fires
Birds
Selected Poems (Australian Poets Series)
Five Senses (Selected Poems)
The Other Half
Collected Poems 1942–1970
Alive: Poems 1971–1972
Fourth Quarter

BIOGRAPHY
The Generations of Men

CRITICISM
Preoccupations in Australian Poetry
Because I Was Invited

The Houghton Mifflin New Poetry Series

Judith Leet, *Pleasure Seeker's Guide*
David St. John, *Hush*
Heather McHugh, *Dangers*
Gerald Stern, *Lucky Life*
Judith Wright, *The Double Tree: Selected Poems 1942–1976*

Judith Wright

The Double Tree

SELECTED POEMS

1942–1976

WITH AN INTRODUCTION BY THE AUTHOR

HOUGHTON MIFFLIN COMPANY
BOSTON 1978

A grant from the Literature Board of the Australia Council has aided the publication of this book.

Library of Congress Cataloging in Publication Data

Wright, Judith.
    The double tree.
        I. Title.
PR9619.3.W7D6   821   78–4261
ISBN 0–395–26480–4
ISBN 0–395–26466–9 pbk.

Printed in the United States of America

W 10 9 8 7 6 5 4 3 2 1

Contents

FROM *The Gateway* (1953)

FROM *Five Senses* (*The Forest*) (1963)

FROM *The Other Half* (1966)

From *Shadow* (1970)

From *Alive: Poems 1971–1972* (1973)

FROM *Fourth Quarter* (1976)

Introduction

*T*HE POEMS selected for this book were written over a span of more than thirty years. My own country and background are significant in many of them, and since these will be unfamiliar to most American readers, the book needs some introduction.

Australia was among the last countries to be annexed by Europeans. Its landscape was wholly unfamiliar to the first settlers, who often felt it hostile, difficult and forbidding. Its first inhabitants, the Australian Aborigines, who had occupied the country at least forty thousand years before, were taken over by the British Crown without benefit of treaties, often with much cruelty, and with a total lack of understanding of their lives and their essential religious bonding with the land. In this takeover, my own ancestors played a part, since they have been pastoralists and land-owners ever since the first of them arrived in 1828.

I myself was born and brought up in the New England country of New South Wales, on a pastoral property. Though it was distant from the nearest town and much more distant from the cities, I was given a university education and afterwards a year's travel in Europe. When I returned, I worked in Sydney for some years, until World War II sent me back to New England to help with the running of the property in the absence of my brothers in the army.

The beauty of that country, then threatened by Japanese invasion, renewed my own bonds with it, and also raised for me the question of white Australians' treatment of the land itself. Eroded soils, the destruction of forests and wildlife, and the forces of change were already apparent everywhere. They were among my father's own concerns, and he taught me to look at the country with seeing eyes.

Later, I went to Brisbane, where I worked in its university, *xiii* helped with the running of a small literary magazine, began to publish my own poetry, and through that met the man who became my husband. Over the next two decades, we lived near Brisbane on a richly forested plateau, had one daughter, and earned our living largely by writing, while I helped him in his major life-task, a study of the development of Western thought.

The years after the war brought an upsurge in national prosperity and an even heavier assault on the country, this time with the aid of bulldozers and aerial agriculture and of much overseas capital for mining and pastoral industry. With others, I founded a society for wildlife conservation, and was its president from 1962 to 1975. We took on many major tasks, including the defence of the Great Barrier Reef, a magnificent stretch of coral reefs and islands off the Queensland coast, against the threats of mining for limestone and drilling for oil, and the attempt to obtain national parks and reserves, in a State which was bent on progress, industrialization, and the furthering of private interests. Working with scientists and ecologists, I had an intensive education in the politics of conservation, which culminated in 1973–74 in membership of a government committee of inquiry. This took me around Australia, observing the havoc we had caused and editing the committee's final report.

All these experiences have contributed to the making of the poems in this book, as well, of course, as my personal life and thought. Poetry cannot be propaganda, but it must spring from the central core of one's living and feeling, so this brief outline may help in interpreting the poems.

Writing poetry has always been to me the most meaningful part of my life, though I have written much in prose, including literary criticism, a biographical novel based on the story of my pioneering forebears, essays and monographs and even a few books for children. This country has a comparatively small audience for writers, and certainly it is as impossible here as anywhere to earn a living as poet. I hope the poems Jonathan Galassi has selected may speak to you not only as a voice from a distant country, but sometimes through aspects of your own being and living.

Judith Wright

The Double Tree

SELECTED POEMS   1942–1976

FROM

The Moving Image

(1946)

The Moving Image

I

Here is the same clock that walked quietly
through those enormous years I half recall,
when between one blue summer and another
time seemed as many miles as round the world,
and world a day, a moment or a mile,
or a sweet slope of grass edged with the sea,
or a new song to sing, or a tree dressed in gold —
time and the world that faster spin until
mind cannot grasp them now or heart take hold.

Only the sound of the clock is still the same.
Each of us followed it to a different hour
that like a bushranger held its guns on us
and forced our choice. And the clock begins to race.
We are caught in the endless circle of time and star
that never chime with the blood; we weary, we grow lame,
stumbling after their incessant pace
that slackens for us only when we are
caught deep in sleep, or music, or a lover's face.

Here where I walk was the green world of a child;
the infinity of day that closed in day,

the widening spiral turning and returning,
the same and not the same, that had no end.
Does the heart know no better than to pray
that time unwind its coil, the bone unbuild
till that lost world sit like a fruit in the hand —
till the felled trees rise upright where they lay
and leaves and birds spring on them as they stand?

And yet, the lovelier distance is ahead.
I would go farther with you, clock and star,
though the earth break under my feet and storm
snatch at my breath and night ride over me.
I am the maker. I have made both time and fear,
knowing that to yield to either is to be dead.
All that is real is to live, to desire, to be,
till I say to the child I was, "It is this; it is here.
In the doomed cell I have found love's whole eternity."

II

Dust blows harsh from the airfield; dust in the mouth.
This is the field that once was the world's end
(nothing beyond but hills water-hyacinth–coloured,
nothing in the field but supplejack and black-sally).
Dust blows back from the airfield; dust on the hand,
dust in the eyes that watch the plane turn north;
and to the plane the hills, the mysterious valley,
are bald and meagre as a map made out of sand —
hills of the wild horses, gullies of the rock-lily.

Looking from so high the world is evil and small
like a dried head from the islands with a grin of shell,
brittle and easy to break. ·But there is no end to the breaking —
one smashed, another mocks from your enemy's eye —
put that out, there's a world in every skull.
Nothing left but to pray, God save us all;
nothing but the tick of the clock and a world sucked dry;
nothing; till the tide of time come back to the full
and drown a man too sane, who climbed too high.

Till the tide of life come back, till time's great tide
roar from our depths and send us mad again
with a singing madness, like poor Tom of Bedlam —
poor Tom, through whose feverish blood life poured like thunder
till the frail floodgates burst within his brain,
and sleepless in his cell he sang and cried;
till the straw of his prison broke into flowers of wonder;
till the universe was the limit of his chain
and galaxies glowed through the low roof he lay under.

All the lives that met in him and made
the tiny world of his life, his passion, his skill
shone for his eyes each as a separate star.
Age upon age of effort and terror and thought
stretched from his birth back to a single cell;
life upon life leapt from the fountaining seed,
lusted and took, hated, delighted and fought,
built from the thread of its dream a heaven and hell,
took up the search of man and died as it sought.

The first birth and the first cry and the first death,
the world of the first cell and the first man,
every sound and motion forgotten, remembered,
left their trace in his body, their voice in his speech.
One word in his mouth spread open like a fan,
the sound of it dwarfed the stars and stole his breath
as a million voices shouted it each to each;
and through the web of all their lives he ran
to grasp a glory never in one man's reach.

Poor Tom, in whose blood's intricate channelled track,
in the unsailed sea of his heart, in his witchball eyes,
in his senses that spoke and mind that shaped a world
passionate terrible love never ceased burning;
who played with comets and stars like golden flies;
whose nights and days were whipmarks on his back,
whose birth and death were the sun and moon returning.
What songs shall a madman sing before he dies,
who makes one word of the song all life is learning?

Over the airfield looms the idol of night.
In its shadow the earth is spun by a stellar wind
in an eddy of spiralled stars. We are dwarfed by the dark.
We inherit a handful of dust and a fragment of stone.
Yet listen, the music grows around us, before us, behind,
there is sound in the silence; the dark is a tremor of light.
It is the corn rising when winter is done.
It is the madmen singing, the lovers, the blind;
the cry of Tom of Bedlam, naked under the sun.

The Company of Lovers

We meet and part now over all the world,
We, the lost company,
take hands together in the night, forget
the night in our brief happiness, silently.
We who sought many things, throw all away
for this one thing, one only,
remembering that in the narrow grave
we shall be lonely.

Death marshals up his armies round us now.
Their footsteps crowd too near.
Lock your warm hand above the chilling heart
and for a time I live without my fear.
Grope in the night to find me and embrace,
for the dark preludes of the drums begin,
and round us, round the company of lovers,
Death draws his cordons in.

Bora Ring

The song is gone; the dance
is secret with the dancers in the earth,
the ritual useless, and the tribal story
lost in an alien tale.

Only the grass stands up
to mark the dancing-ring: the apple-gums
posture and mime a past corroboree,
murmur a broken chant.

The hunter is gone: the spear
is splintered underground; the painted bodies
a dream the world breathed sleeping and forgot.
The nomad feet are still.

Only the rider's heart
halts at a sightless shadow, an unsaid word
that fastens in the blood the ancient curse,
the fear as old as Cain.

Waiting

Day's crystal hemisphere travels the land.
From starfrost to starfrost the folded hills lie bare
and the sheep move grazing or stand.
How can the sirens of danger pierce this air?
Only the parrots exploding in green and scarlet
shatter its glass for their shrill moment's flight.
From the houses on the hill the small smoke rises
in patterns of vague peace from dawn to night.

But the circling days weave tighter, and the spider
Time binds us helpless till his sting go in.
Moving in a dazed routine, we hardly wonder

what hour ahead waits with a basilisk grin.
Only the radio, like a seashell held to the ear,
gives back the echo of our own blood's fever;
its confused voices like the body's urgent warning
of a disease that it may not recover.

Oh, let time be only the monster of a dream,
the sick distortion of minds anaesthetised;
let time be only the calm surgeon, deciding
our cancer is not mortal, can be excised.
But past our prayers we know only ourselves
have choice or power to make us whole again;
time lifts no knives to heal or to destroy,
and did not cause, and cannot cure, our pain.

All that time gives is the crystal hour of waiting
through which we travel, listening to the radio
turn back ourselves upon us; our own Iscariots,
we know the agony we do not know.
The witchball hour returns the twisted face
of what we are; oh, let our weeping be
amendment for these lives, and make us whole
in man and time, who build eternity.

Remittance Man

The spendthrift, disinherited and graceless,
accepted his pittance with an easy air,
only surprised he could escape so simply
from the pheasant-shooting and the aunts in the close;
took to the life, dropped easily out of knowledge,
and tramping the backtracks in the summer haze
let everything but life slip through his fingers.

Blue blowing smoke of twigs from the noon fire,
red blowing dust of roads where the teams go slow,
sparse swinging shadow of trees no longer foreign

silted the memory of a greener climate.
The crazy tales, the hatters' crazy secrets,
the blind-drunk sprees indifferently forgiven,
and past them all, the track to escape and nowhere
suited his book, the freak who could never settle.
That pale stalk of a wench at the county ball
sank back forgotten in black Mary's eyes,
and past the sallow circle of the plains' horizon
faded the rainy elms seen through the nursery window.

That harsh biblical country of the scapegoat
closed its magnificence finally round his bones
polished by diligent ants. The squire his brother,
presuming death, sighed over the documents,
and lifting his eyes across the inherited garden
let a vague pity blur the formal roses.

The Trains

Tunnelling through the night, the trains pass
in a splendour of power, with a sound like thunder
shaking the orchards, waking
the young from a dream, scattering like glass
the old men's sleep; laying
a black trail over the still bloom of the orchards.
The trains go north with guns.

Strange primitive piece of flesh, the heart laid quiet
hearing their cry pierce through its thin-walled cave
recalls the forgotten tiger
and leaps awake in its old panic riot;
and how shall mind be sober,
since blood's red thread still binds us fast in history?
Tiger, you walk through all our past and future,
troubling the children's sleep; laying
a reeking trail across our dream of orchards.

Racing on iron errands, the trains go by,
and over the white acres of our orchards
hurl their wild summoning cry, their animal cry . . .
the trains go north with guns.

Sonnet

Now let the draughtsman of my eyes be done
marking the line of petal and of hill.
Let the long commentary of the brain
be silent. Evening and the earth are one,
and bird and tree are simple and stand still.
Now, fragile heart swung in your webs of vein,
and perilous self won hardly out of clay,
gather the harvest of last light, and reap
the luminous fields of sunset for your bread.
Blurs the laborious focus of the day
and shadow brims the hillside slow as sleep.
Here is the word that, when all words are said,
shall compass more than speech. The sun is gone;
draws on the night at last; the dream draws on.

Bullocky

Beside his heavy-shouldered team,
thirsty with drought and chilled with rain,
he weathered all the striding years
till they ran widdershins in his brain:

Till the long solitary tracks
etched deeper with each lurching load
were populous before his eyes,
and fiends and angels used his road.

All the long straining journey grew
a mad apocalyptic dream,
and he old Moses, and the slaves
his suffering and stubborn team.

Then in his evening camp beneath
the half-light pillars of the trees
he filled the steepled cone of night
with shouted prayers and prophecies.

While past the campfire's crimson ring
the star-struck darkness cupped him round,
and centuries of cattlebells
rang with their sweet uneasy sound.

Grass is across the waggon-tracks,
and plough strikes bone beneath the grass,
and vineyards cover all the slopes
where the dead teams were used to pass.

O vine, grow close upon that bone
and hold it with your rooted hand.
The prophet Moses feeds the grape,
and fruitful is the Promised Land.

Brother and Sisters

The road turned out to be a cul-de-sac;
stopped like a lost intention at the gate
and never crossed the mountains to the coast.
But they stayed on. Years grew like grass and leaves
across the half-erased and dubious track
until one day they know the plans were lost,
the blue-print for the bridge was out of date,
and now their orchards never would be planted.
The saplings sprouted slyly; day by day
the bush moved one step nearer, wondering when.

The polished parlour grew distrait and haunted
where Millie, Lucy, John each night at ten
wound the gilt clock that leaked the year away.

The pianola — oh, listen to the mocking-bird —
wavers on Sundays and has lost a note.
The wrinkled ewes snatch pansies through the fence
and stare with shallow eyes into the garden
where Lucy shrivels waiting for a word,
and Millie's cameos loosen round her throat.
The bush comes near, the ranges grow immense.

Feeding the lambs deserted in early spring
Lucy looked up and saw the stockman's eye
telling her she was cracked and old.
                                        The wall
groans in the night and settles more awry.
O how they lie awake. Their thoughts go fluttering
from room to room like moths: "Millie, are you awake?"
"Oh John, I have been dreaming." "Lucy, do you cry?"
— meet tentative as moths. Antennae stroke a wing.
"There is nothing to be afraid of. Nothing at all."

South of My Days

South of my days' circle, part of my blood's country,
rises that tableland, high delicate outline
of bony slopes wincing under the winter,
low trees blue-leaved and olive, outcropping granite —
clean, lean, hungry country. The creek's leaf-silenced,
willow-choked, the slope a tangle of medlar and crabapple
branching over and under, blotched with a green lichen;
and the old cottage lurches in for shelter.

O cold the black-frost night. The walls draw in to the warmth
and the old roof cracks its joints; the slung kettle
hisses a leak on the fire. Hardly to be believed that summer

will turn up again some day in a wave of rambler roses,
thrust its hot face in here to tell another yarn —
a story old Dan can spin into a blanket against the winter.
Seventy years of stories he clutches round his bones.
Seventy summers are hived in him like old honey.

Droving that year, Charleville to the Hunter,
nineteen-one it was, and the drought beginning;
sixty head left at the McIntyre, the mud round them
hardened like iron; and the yellow boy died
in the sulky ahead with the gear, but the horse went on,
stopped at the Sandy Camp and waited in the evening.
It was the flies we seen first, swarming like bees.
Came to the Hunter, three hundred head of a thousand —
cruel to keep them alive — and the river was dust.

Or mustering up in the Bogongs in the autumn
when the blizzards came early. Brought them down; we brought
    them
down, what aren't there yet. Or driving for Cobb's on the run
up from Tamworth — Thunderbolt at the top of Hungry Hill,
and I give him a wink. I wouldn't wait long, Fred,
not if I was you; the troopers are just behind,
coming for that job at the Hillgrove. He went like a luny,
him on his big black horse.

                    Oh, they slide and they vanish
as he shuffles the years like a pack of conjuror's cards.
True or not, it's all the same; and the frost on the roof
cracks like a whip, and the back-log breaks into ash.
Wake, old man. This is winter, and the yarns are over.
No one is listening.
                    South of my days' circle
I know it dark against the stars, the high lean country
full of old stories that still go walking in my sleep.

The Surfer

He thrust his joy against the weight of the sea;
climbed through, slid under those long banks of foam —
(hawthorn hedges in spring, thorns in the face stinging).
How his brown strength drove through the hollow and coil
of green-through weirs of water!
Muscle of arm thrust down long muscle of water;
and swimming so, went out of sight
where mortal, masterful, frail, the gulls went wheeling
in air as he in water, with delight.

Turn home, the sun goes down; swimmer, turn home.
Last leaf of gold vanishes from the sea-curve.
Take the big roller's shoulder, speed and swerve;
come to the long beach home like a gull diving.

For on the sand the grey-wolf sea lies snarling,
cold twilight wind splits the waves' hair and shows
the bones they worry in their wolf-teeth. O, wind blows
and sea crouches on sand, fawning and mouthing;
drops there and snatches again, drops and again snatches
its broken toys, its whitened pebbles and shells.

For New England

Your trees, the homesick and the swarthy native,
blow all one way to me, this southern weather
that smells of early snow:
                     And I remember
The house closed in with sycamore and chestnut
fighting the foreign wind.
Here I will stay, she said; be done with the black north,
the harsh horizon rimmed with drought. —
Planted the island there and drew it round her.
Therefore I find in me the double tree.

And therefore I, deserted on the wharves,
have watched the ships fan out their web of streamers
(thinking of how the lookout at the heads
leaned out towards the dubious rims of sea
to find a sail blown over like a message
you are not forgotten),
or followed through the taproot of the poplar . . .
But look, oh look, the Gothic tree's on fire
with blown galahs, and fuming with wild wings.

The hard inquiring wind strikes to the bone
and whines division.
                  Many roads meet here
in me, the traveller and the ways I travel.
All the hills' gathered waters feed my seas
who am the swimmer and the mountain river;
and the long slopes' concurrence is my flesh
who am the gazer and the land I stare on;
and dogwood blooms within my winter blood,
and orchards fruit in me and need no season.
But sullenly the jealous bones recall
what other earth is shaped and hoarded in them.

Where's home, Ulysses? Cuckolded by lewd time
he never found again the girl he sailed from,
but at his fireside met the islands waiting
and died there, twice a stranger.
                      Wind, blow through me
till the nostalgic candles of laburnum
fuse with the dogwood in a single flame
to touch alight these sapless memories.
Then will my land turn sweetly from the plough
and all my pastures rise as green as spring.

Dust

This sick dust, spiralling with the wind,
is harsh as grief's taste in our mouths
and has eclipsed the small sun.
The remnant earth turns evil,
the steel-shocked earth has turned against the plough
and runs with wind all day, and all night
sighs in our sleep against the windowpane.

Wind was kinder once, carrying cloud
like a waterbag on his shoulder; sun was kinder,
hardening the good wheat brown as a strong man.
Earth was kinder, suffering fire and plough,
breeding the unaccustomed harvest.
Leaning in our doorway together
watching the birdcloud shadows,
the fleetwing windshadows travel our clean wheat
we thought ourselves rich already.
We counted the beautiful money
and gave it in our hearts to the child asleep,
who must never break his body
against the plough and the stubborn rock and tree.

But the wind rises; but the earth rises,
running like an evil river; but the sun grows small,
and when we turn to each other, our eyes are dust
and our words dust.
Dust has overtaken our dreams that were
wider and richer than wheat under the sun,
and war's eroding gale scatters our sons
with a million other grains of dust.

O sighing at the blistered door, darkening the evening star,
the dust accuses. Our dream was the wrong dream,
our strength was the wrong strength.
Weary as we are, we must make a new choice,
a choice more difficult than resignation,

more urgent than our desire of rest at the end of the day.
We must prepare the land for a difficult sowing,
a long and hazardous growth of a strange bread,
that our son's sons may harvest and be fed.

FROM

Woman to Man

(1949)

Woman to Man

The eyeless labourer in the night,
the selfless, shapeless seed I hold,
builds for its resurrection day —
silent and swift and deep from sight
foresees the unimagined light.

This is no child with a child's face;
this has no name to name it by:
yet you and I have known it well.
This is our hunter and our chase,
the third who lay in our embrace.

This is the strength that your arm knows,
the arc of flesh that is my breast,
the precise crystals of our eyes.
This is the blood's wild tree that grows
the intricate and folded rose.

This is the maker and the made;
this is the question and reply;
the blind head butting at the dark,
the blaze of light along the blade.
Oh hold me, for I am afraid.

Woman's Song

O move in me, my darling,
for now the sun must rise;
the sun that will draw open
the lids upon your eyes.

O wake in me, my darling.
The knife of day is bright
to cut the thread that binds you
within the flesh of night.

Today I lose and find you
whom yet my blood would keep —
would weave and sing around you
the spells and songs of sleep.

None but I shall know you
as none but I have known;
yet there's a death and a maiden
who wait for you alone;

so move in me, my darling,
whose debt I cannot pay.
Pain and the dark must claim you,
and passion and the day.

Woman to Child

You who were darkness warmed my flesh
where out of darkness rose the seed.
Then all a world I made in me;
all the world you hear and see
hung upon my dreaming blood.

There moved the multitudinous stars,
and coloured birds and fishes moved.
There swam the sliding continents.
All time lay rolled in me, and sense,
and love that knew not its beloved.

O node and focus of the world;
I hold you deep within that well
you shall escape and not escape —
that mirrors still your sleeping shape;
that nurtures still your crescent cell.

I wither and you break from me;
yet though you dance in living light
I am the earth, I am the root,
I am the stem that fed the fruit,
the link that joins you to the night.

The Maker

I hold the crimson fruit
and plumage of the palm;
flame-tree, that scarlet spirit,
in my soil takes root.

My days burn with the sun,
my nights with moon and star,
since into myself I took
all living things that are.

All things that glow and move,
all things that change and pass,
I gather their delight
as in a burning-glass;

all things I focus in
the crystal of my sense.
I give them breath and life
and set them free in the dance.

I am a tranquil lake
to mirror their joy and pain;
and all their pain and joy
I from my own heart make,

since love, who cancels fear
with his fixèd will,
burned my vision clear
and bid my sense be still.

Child and Wattle-Tree

Round as a sun is the golden tree.
Its honey dust sifts down among the light
to cover me and my hot blood
and my heart hiding like a sad bird
among its birds and shadows.

Lock your branches around me, tree;
let the harsh wooden scales of bark enclose me.
Take me into your life and smother me with bloom
till my feet are cool in the earth
and my hair is long in the wind;
till I am a golden tree spinning the sunlight.

Strong as the sun is the golden tree
that gives and says nothing,
that takes and knows nothing;
but I am stronger than the sun; I am a child.
The tree I am lying beneath is the tree of my heart,
and my heart moves like a dark bird
among its birds and shadows.   *19*

Spring after War

Winter and spring the clouds drift in,
and mist is grey as moving sheep
where ewe goes heavy in lamb, and ewe
beside her lamb lies half-asleep,
her narrow sides with milk drawn thin.

How reconcile the alien eyes,
the warring life how reconcile?
On the lean slope and dripping hill
the sheep move slowly, single-file.
Where is it the heart's country lies?

The rope-vines hang where the clouds move.
The scorpion dances in the brain.
The years of death rattle their bones.
The ewe cries in the pitiless rain
the mortal cry of anguished love.

Which is the country, which is true?
How reconcile the treacherous earth,
the gaping flesh how reconcile —
and still move forward to some birth,
as the lamb moves within the ewe?

Within the bones the scorpion lay.
Within the bones the lamb was made.
Within the bones the heart is housed.
The blood that leaps behind the blade
is death or life; is night or day.

The knife goes back into its sheath;
the lamb comes struggling from the womb:
the seeking flesh has found its goal.
The compass heart swings seeking home
between the lands of life and death.

The Child

To be alone in a strange place in spring
shakes the heart. The others are somewhere else;
the shouting, the running, the eating, the drinking —
never alone and thinking,
never remembering the Dream or finding the Thing,
always striving with your breath hardly above the water.
But to go away, to be quiet and go away,
to be alone in a strange place in spring
shakes the heart.

To hide in a thrust of green leaves
with the blood's leap and retreat
warm in you;
burning, going and returning
like a thrust of green leaves
out of your eyes, out of your hands and your feet —
like a noise of bees, growing, increasing;
to turn and to look up,
to find above you the enfolding, the exulting
may-tree
shakes the heart.

Spring is always the red tower of the may-tree,
alive, shaken with bees, smelling of wild honey,
and the blood a moving tree of may;
like a symbol for a meaning; like time's recurrent morning
that breaks and beckons, changes and eludes,
that is gone away;
that is never gone away.

Camphor Laurel

Here in the slack of night
the tree breathes honey and moonlight.
Here in the blackened yard

smoke and time and use have marred,
leaning from that fantan gloom
the bent tree is heavy in bloom.

The dark house creaks and sways;
"Not like the old days."
Tim and Sam and ragbag Nell,
Wong who keeps the Chinese hell,
the half-caste lovers, the humpbacked boy,
sleep for sorrow or wake for joy.

Under the house the roots go deep,
down, down, while the sleepers sleep;
splitting the rock where the house is set,
cracking the paved and broken street.
Old Tim turns and old Sam groans,
"God be good to my breaking bones";
and in the slack of tideless night
the tree breathes honey and moonlight.

The World and the Child

I

This is the child. He has not yet put out leaves.
His bare skin tastes the air; his naked eyes
know nothing but strange shapes. Nothing is named;
nothing is ago, nothing not yet. Death is that which dies,
and goes no farther; for the mere dead he grieves,
and grief has yet no meaning and no size.

Where the wild harebell grows to a blue cave
and the climbing ant is a monster of green light
the child clings to his grassblade. The mountain range
lies like a pillow for his head at night,
the moon swings from his ceiling. He is a wave
that timeless moves through time, imperishably bright.

Yet what it is that moves? What is the unresting hunger
that shapes the soft-fleshed face, makes the bones harden?
Rebel, rebel, it cries. Never be satisfied.
Do not weaken for their grief; do not give in or pardon.
Only through this pain, this black desire, this anger,
shall you at last return to your lost garden.

II

Out of himself like a thread the child spins pain
and makes a net to catch the unknown world.
Words gather there heavy as fish, and tears,
and tales of love and of the polar cold.
Now, says the child, I shall never be young again.
The shadow of my net has darkened the sea's gold.

Yet what is it that draws the net and throws?
Forget to be young, it says; forget to be afraid.
No net is strong enough to hold the world,
nor man of such a sinew ever was made.
What is the world? That secret no man knows:
yet look, beyond the sundazzle, the blinding blade —
was not that the white waterfall from some vast side?

Nets have been breached and men have died in vain.
No net is strong enough to hold the world.
Yet gather in your bleeding hands your net again —
not till Leviathan's beached shall you be satisfied.

Night after Bushfire

There is no more silence on the plains of the moon
and time is no more alien there, than here.
Sun thrust his warm hand down at the high noon,
but all that stirred was the faint dust of fear.

Charred death upon the rock leans his charred bone
and stares at death from sockets black with flame.
Man, if he come to brave that glance alone,
must leave behind his human home and name.

Carry like a threatened thing your soul away,
and do not look too long to left or right,
for he whose soul wears the strict chains of day
will lose it in this landscape of charcoal and moonlight.

.

Dream

Travelling through a strange night by a strange light
I sought upon the hill the crimson rose
that without age and in no acre grows;
and I was caught by silence at that sight.

The burning wires of nerves, the crimson way
from head to heart, the towering tree of blood —
who travels here must move, not as he would,
but fed and lit by love alone he may.

O dying tree, I move beneath your shade;
and road of blood, I travel where you lead;
and rose unseen, upon your thorn I bleed;
and in a triple dream a dream I made.

I travel through this night and by this light
to find upon a hill the unsought rose
that out of silence into silence grows;
and silence overtakes me at that sight.

The Cycads

Their smooth dark flames flicker at time's own root.
Round them the rising forests of the years
alter the climates of forgotten earth
and silt with leaves the strata of first birth.

Only the antique cycads sullenly
keep the old bargain life has long since broken;
and, cursed by age, through each chill century
they watch the shrunken moon, but never die,

for time forgets the promise he once made,
and change forgets that they are left alone.
Among the complicated birds and flowers
they seem a generation carved in stone.

Leaning together, down those gulfs they stare
over whose darkness dance the brilliant birds
that cry in air one moment, and are gone;
and with their countless suns the years spin on.

Take their cold seed and set it in the mind,
and its slow root will lengthen deep and deep
till, following, you cling on the last ledge
over the unthinkable, unfathomed edge
beyond which man remembers only sleep.

The Twins

Not because of their beauty — though they are slender
as saplings of white cedar, and long as lilies —
not because of their delicate dancing step
or their brown hair sideways blown like the manes of fillies —
it is not for their beauty that the crowd in the street

wavers like dry leaves around them on the wind.
It is the chord, the intricate unison
of one and one, strikes home to the watcher's mind.

How sweet is the double gesture, the mirror-answer;
same hand woven in same, like arm in arm.
Salt blood like tears freshens the crowd's dry veins,
and moving in its web of time and harm
the unloved heart asks, "Where is my reply,
my kin, my answer? I am driven and alone."
Their serene eyes seek nothing. They walk by.
They move into the future and are gone.

Eli, Eli

To see them go by drowning in the river —
soldiers and elders drowning in the river,
the pitiful women drowning in the river,
the children's faces staring from the river —
that was his cross, and not the cross they gave him.

To hold the invisible wand, and not to save them —
to know them turned to death, and yet not save them;
only to cry to them and not to save them,
knowing that no one but themselves could save them —
this was the wound, more than the wound they dealt him.

To hold out love and know they would not take it,
to hold out faith and know they dared not take it —
the invisible wand, and none would see or take it,
all he could give, and there was none to take it —
thus they betrayed him, not with the tongue's betrayal.

He watched, and they were drowning in the river;
faces like sodden flowers in the river —
faces of children moving in the river;
and all the while, he knew there was no river.

26

The Builders

Only those coral insects live
that work and endure under
the breakers' cold continual thunder.
They are the quick of the reef
that rots and crumbles in a calmer water.
Only those men survive
who dare to hold their love against the world;
who dare to live and doubt what they are told.
They are the quick of life;
their faith is insolence; joyful is their grief.

This is life's promise and accomplishment —
a fraction-foothold taken.
Where dark eroding seas had broken,
the quick, the sensitive, the lover,
the passionate touch and intergrowth of living.
Alive, alive, intent,
love rises on the crumbling shells it shed.
The strata of the dead
burst with the plumes and passions of the earth.
Seed falls there now, birds build, and life takes over.

The Mirror at the Fun Fair

This dark grotesque, this my familiar double
I meet again among the lights and sawdust.
This is the changeling head that weights my shoulders,
the sidelong china smile that masks my trouble:
and there is no escape in the brass music,
no loss of self among the moving crowd.
Ah, my clown-lover, how shall we dissemble?

I do not fear the small rat-teeth of time
that gnaw my matchwood beauty. I do not fear
the splintering blow of death who waits behind me.

These are the foe, the faces in this frame,
the twisted images that from the mirror
grimace like hatred, wrenching us awry
till love's a club-foot pander, sly and lame.

Look in the mirror. Silent, unleashed and savage,
the nameless crowd sways in its coil and waits.
Look, we are caught; look, we are lost and homeless.
The gunman crowd watches to do us damage.
The crowd repeats, repeats our crooked faces;
our bird-thin hands, our desperate eyes that stare,
and, "Hate," each lover cries to his companion.
"O hate that is my pain. O desolate fear."

Night

Standing here in the night
we are turned to a great tree,
every leaf a star,
its root eternity.

So deeply goes its root
into the world's womb,
so high rises its stem
it leaves for death no room.

We are turned to a great tree
hung with heavy fruit,
torn by the winds of time
and the worm at the root.

Come back to the kind flesh,
to love and simple sight.
Let us forget awhile
that we create the night;

Out of this dark of time
alive and human, come.
Brief is the warm day
wherein we have our home.

The Killer

The day was clear as fire,
the birds sang frail as glass,
when thirsty I came to the creek
and fell by its side in the grass.

My breast on the bright moss
and shower-embroidered weeds,
my lips to the live water
I saw him turn in the reeds.

Black horror sprang from the dark
in a violent birth,
and through its cloth of grass
I felt the clutch of earth.

O beat him into the ground.
O strike him till he dies,
or else your life itself
drains through those colourless eyes.

I struck again and again.
Slender in black and red
he lies, and his icy glance
turns outward, clear and dead.

But nimble my enemy
as water is, or wind.
He has slipped from his death aside
and vanished into my mind.

He has vanished whence he came,
my nimble enemy;
and the ants come out to the snake
and drink at his shallow eye.

Midnight

Darkness where I find my sight,
shadowless and burning night,
here where death and life are met
is the fire of being set.

Watchman eye and workman hand
are spun of water, air and sand.
These will crumble and be gone,
still that darkness rages on.

As a plant in winter dies
down into the germ, and lies
leafless, tongueless, lost in earth
imaging its fierce rebirth;

And with the whirling rays of the sun
and shuttle-stroke of living rain
weaves that image from its heart
and like a god is born again —

so let my blood reshape its dream,
drawn into that tideless stream;
that shadowless and burning night
of darkness where I find my sight.

Wonga Vine

Look down; be still.
The sunburst day's on fire,
O twilight bell,
flower of the wonga vine.

I gather you
out of his withering light.
Sleep there, red;
sleep there, yellow and white.

Move as the creek
moves to its hidden pool.
The sun has eyes of fire;
be my white waterfall.

Lie on my eyes like hands,
let no sun shine —
O twilight bell,
flower of the wonga vine.

Night and the Child

In the morning the hawk and the sun flew up together;
the wildhaired sun and the wild bird of prey.
Now both are fallen out of the treacherous sky.
One holds a bullet as leaden as the lid of his eye
and one from the west's red beaches fell to the western water.
O hawk and sun of my morning, how far you are gone down.

The night comes up over you, faceless and forbidden,
over the hawk sunk in earth and the sun drunk by the sea;
and who can tell, the child said, no matter what they say —
who can be sure that the sun will rise on another day?   *31*

For he died in his blood on the water as the hawk died, and is
    hidden.
How far under the grey eyelid the yellow eye is gone.

Who can be sure, the child said, that there will be a waking?
Now I am given to the night and my soul is afraid.
I would people the dark with candles and friends to stay by my
    side
but the darkness said, Only in my heart can you hide.
I said to the dark, Be my friend; but the dark said, I am nothing,
and now I must turn my face to the sea of Nothing and drown.

And no one could reach me or save me out of that deadly dream
until deep under the sea I found the sleeping sun.
With the sun asleep in my arms I sank and was not and was
    gone
even as the hawk was gone after the noise of the gun.
I who run on the beach where the morning sun is warm
went under the black sea, and rose with the sun, and am born.

The Blind Man

I. The Dust in the Township

Under the Moreton Bay fig by the war memorial
blind Jimmy Delaney sits alone and sings
in the pollen-coloured dust; and Jimmy Delaney
coloured like the dust, is of that dust
three generations made. Sing for the dust
then, Jimmy, thin and strange as old fiddle-strings
or the dry wires of grass-stems stretched in the thrust
of a winter westerly; and if it's true
black Mary's your father's mother, none better than you
can speak in the voice of the forgotten dust.

Horrie Delaney came here first with cattle,
and shook the dust out of its golden sleep;
the golden sleep of eternal generation.

Grass, wattle- and messmate-tree and earth;
death bearing life, and both come out of earth.
Deeper than the shadows of trees and tribes, deep
lay the spring that issued in death and birth.
Horrie Delaney with his dogs and his gun
came like another shadow between the earth and the sun
and now with the tribes he is gone down in death.

Dick Delaney the combo cleared these hills.
Easily the bush fell and lightly, now it seems
to us who forget the sweat of Dick Delaney,
and the humpy and the scalding sunlight and the black
hate between the white skin and the black.
The smoke sang upward, the trees vanished like dreams
and the long hills lie naked as a whipped back.
Greed and hunger tear at the marrow-bone
and the heart in the breast hangs heavy as a great gold stone.
Under the marred earth, his bones twist on that rack.

Yellow Delaney is the third of that name
and like the yellow dust, he finds no rest.
Landless and loveless he went wandering
with his despised white girl, and left no track
but the black mark of a campfire. How can they die
who live without a country? He does not die
though like the night curlew the blood mourns in his breast
and gets no answer. Under the tenantless sky
he lives by his traps in the lost ranges; he
is the brain-fever bird calling from a rung tree
that time is a cracked mask and day a golden lie.

Under the Moreton Bay fig by the war memorial
Jimmy Delaney the blind man sits and sings
where the wind raises dry fountains of faded gold.
No one has loved or sung of the unregarded dust.
Dance upright in the wind, dry-voiced and humble dust
out of whose breast the great green fig-tree springs,
and the proud man, and the singer, and the outcast.
All are but shadows between the earth and the sun
sings Jimmy Delaney, sitting where the dust-whirls run,
columns of dancing dust that sink at last.

33

And yet those men, this fallen dust, these shadows
remembered only by the blind man whose songs none hear
sting him in the noon sunlight as a hornet stings.
The conqueror who possessed a world alone,
and he who hammered a world on his heart's stone,
and last the man whose world splintered in fear —
their shadows lengthen in the light of noon;
their dust bites deep, driven by a restless wind.
O singer, son of darkness, love that is blind,
sing for the golden dust that dances and is gone.

II. COUNTRY DANCE

The dance in the township hall is nearly over.
Hours ago the stiff-handed wood-cheeked women
got up from the benches round the walls
and took home their aching eyes and weary children.
Mrs McLarty with twenty cows to milk
before dawn, went with the music stinging
like sixty wasps under her best dress.
Eva Callaghan whose boy died in the army
sat under the streamers like a house to let
and went alone, a black pot brimming with tears.
"Once my body was a white cedar, my breasts the buds on the
     quince-tree,
that now are fallen and grey like logs on a cleared hill.
Then why is my blood not quiet? what is the good
of the whips of music stinging along my blood?"

The dance in the township hall is nearly over.
Outside in the yard the fire like a great red city
eats back into the log, its noisy flames fallen.
Jimmy Dunn has forgotten his camp in the hills
and sleeps like a heap of rags beside a bottle.
The young boys sit and stare at the heart of the city
thinking of the neon lights and the girls at the corners
with lips like coals and thighs as silver as florins.
Jock Hamilton thinks of the bally cow gone sick
and the cockatoos in the corn and the corn ready to pick
and the wires in the thirty-acre broken.

Oh, what rats nibble at the cords of our nerves?
When will the wires break, the ploughed paddocks lie open,
the bow of the fiddle saw through the breast-bone,
the dream be done, and we waken?

Streamers and boughs are falling, the dance grows faster.
Only the lovers and the young are dancing
now at the end of the dance, in a trance or singing.
Say the lovers locked together and crowned with coloured paper:
"The bit of black glass I picked up out of the campfire
is the light that the moon puts on your hair."
"The green pool I swam in under the willows
is the drowning depth, the summer night of your eyes."
"You are the death I move to." "O burning weapon,
you are the pain I long for."

Stars, leaves and streamers fall in the dark dust
and the blind man lies alone in his sphere of night.

Oh, I,
red centre of a dark and burning sky,
fit my words to music, my crippled words to music,
and sing to the fire with the voice of the fire.
Go sleep with your grief, go sleep with your desire,
go deep into the core of night and silence.
But I hold all of it, your hate and sorrow,
your passion and your fear; I am the breath
that holds you from your death.
I am the voice of music and the ended dance.

III. The Singer to the Child

I cannot tell your voice from the voice of the dust,
the stinging river of drought that runs with the wind;
for the dust cries with a child's voice as it goes past,
telling of the blood that falls, and the death of the mind.
If you would speak to me, do not forget I am blind.

I am the singing man who pours dust in the palm of his hand.
It is as dark as dry blood or as bright as the dust of gold.
I do not need to know the colours of earth, who am blind.

Your voice is the voice of the dust that weeps at the world's
    end —
of a child among violent masks, weeping the death of the world.

Who will gather the dust to a sphere, who will build us a world?
Who will join atom to atom, the waiting seed to the seed?
Who will give the heat of the sun to death's great grave of cold,
and deliver the countries of the heart, in the womb of a dust-
    grain furled?
Who will join lover to loved, and raise from the ash the blazing
    bird?

We two, the singer and the crying child, must feed
that whirling phantom on the wind of the world's end.
Only these two can join the sperm to the golden seed —
the tears of a child that fall for the dust at the world's end
and the song of the singer of love, whom the wasps of the dust
    made blind.

IV. Lost Child

Is the boy lost? Then I know where he is gone.
He has gone climbing the terrible crags of the Sun.

The searchers go through the green valley, shouting his name;
the dogs are moaning on the hill for the scent of his track;
but the men will all be hoarse and the dogs lame
before the Hamiltons' boy is found or comes back.
Through the smouldering ice of the moon he is stumbling alone.
I shall rise from my dark and follow where he is gone.

I heard from my bed his bugle breath go by
and the drum of his heart in the measure of an old song.
I shall travel into silence, and in that fierce country
when we meet he will know he has been away too long.
They are looking for him now in the vine-scrub over the hill,
but I think he is alone in a place that I know well.

Is the boy lost? Then I know where he is gone.
He is climbing to Paradise up a river of stars and stone.

V. BLIND MAN'S SONG

No one but a child or a fool dares
to listen to silence, or to the words of this song.
Silence goes back into the man who hears
and carries all the sorrow was ever in his ears
and all the fear he has gathered all his life long:
and this song is a fool's song.

The old man and the young man saw me lie
like a yellow snake in the dust when the dust was still.
The whispering song of the wind or the snake sang I
and the old man turned his head away and went by,
and the young man set his horse full speed at the hill;
but the song went on still.

I have the tune of the singer who makes men afraid.
I repeat the small speech of the worm in the ground,
and out of the depths of the rock my words are made.
I have laid my ear to the dust, and the thing it said
was Silence. Therefore I have made silence speak; I found
for the night a sound.

So no one but a fool or a lonely child
will turn his head to listen to my song.
I am the yellow snake with a dark, a double tongue,
speaking from the dust to the two rulers of the world.

FROM

The Gateway

(1953)

Train Journey

Glassed with cold sleep and dazzled by the moon,
out of the confused hammering dark of the train
I looked and saw under the moon's cold sheet
your delicate dry breasts, country that built my heart;

and the small trees on their uncoloured slope
like poetry moved, articulate and sharp
and purposeful under the great dry flight of air,
under the crosswise currents of wind and star.

Clench down your strength, box-tree and ironbark.
Break with your violent root the virgin rock.
Draw from the flying dark its breath of dew
till the unliving come to life in you.

Be over the blind rock a skin of sense,
under the barren height a slender dance . . .

I woke and saw the dark small trees that burn
suddenly into flowers more lovely than the white moon.

Eroded Hills

These hills my father's father stripped,
and beggars to the winter wind
they crouch like shoulders naked and whipped —
humble, abandoned, out of mind.

Of their scant creeks I drank once
and ate sour cherries from old trees
found in their gullies fruiting by chance.
Neither fruit nor water gave my mind ease.

I dream of hills bandaged in snow,
their eyelids clenched to keep out fear.
When the last leaf and bird go
let my thoughts stand like trees here.

Old House

Where now outside the weary house the pepperina,
that great broken tree, gropes with its blind hands
and sings a moment in the magpie's voice, there he stood once,
that redhaired man my great-great-grandfather,
his long face amiable as an animal's,
and thought of vines and horses.
He moved in that mindless country like a red ant,
running tireless in the summer heat among the trees —
the nameless trees, the sleeping soil, the original river —
and said that the eastern slope would do for a vineyard.

In the camp by the river they made up songs about him,
songs about the waggons, songs about the cattle,
songs about the horses and the children and the woman.
These were a dream, something strayed out of a dream.
They would vanish down the river, but the river would flow on,
under the river-oaks the river would flow on,

winter and summer would burn the grass white
or red like the red of the pale man's hair.
In the camp by the river they made up those songs
and my great-great-grandfather heard them with one part of his
 mind.

And in those days
there was one of him and a thousand of them,
and in these days none are left —
neither a pale man with kangaroo-grass hair
nor a camp of dark singers mocking by the river.
And the trees and the creatures, all of them are gone.
But the sad river, the silted river,
under its dark banks the river flows on,
the wind still blows and the river still flows.
And the great broken tree, the dying pepperina,
clutches in its hands the fragments of a song.

Drought Year

That time of drought the embered air
burned to the roots of timber and grass.
The crackling lime-scrub would not bear
and Mooni Creek was sand that year.
The dingoes' cry was strange to hear.

I heard the dingoes cry
in the whipstick scrub on the Thirty-mile Dry.
I saw the wagtail take his fill
perching in the seething skull.
I saw the eel wither where he curled
in the last blood-drop of a spent world.

I heard the bone whisper in the hide
of the big red horse that lay where he died.
Prop that horse up, make him stand,

hoofs turned down in the bitter sand —
make him stand at the gate of the Thirty-mile Dry.
Turn this way and you will die —
and strange and loud was the dingoes' cry.

Flood Year

Walking up the driftwood beach at day's end
I saw it, thrust up out of a hillock of sand —
a frail bleached clench of fingers dried by wind —
the dead child's hand.

And they are mourning there still, though I forget,
the year of flood, the scoured ruined land,
the herds gone down the current, the farms drowned,
and the child never found.

When I was there the thick hurling waters
had gone back to the river, the farms were almost drained.
Banished half-dead cattle searched the dunes; it rained;
river and sea met with a wild sound.

Oh with a wild sound water flung into air
where sea met river; all the country round
no heart was quiet. I walked on the driftwood sand
and saw the pale crab crouched, and came to a stand
thinking, A child's hand. The child's hand.

Botanical Gardens

Under the miraculous baptism of fire
that bows the poinciana tree, the old man drab as a grub
burrows with his spade. Alas, one's whole life long
to be haunted by these visions of fulfilled desire.

"Alas," he cries, leaning alone on the wet bar of the pub,
"to find them flourishing, clambering, gesturing in the mind —
the sweet white flesh of lilies, the clutching lips of the vine,
the naked flame-trees, their dark limbs curved and strong.

"Oh terrible garden to which my small grey life is food —
oh innocent passionate stare recurring year after year.
Great purple clematis, cassias draped in their golden hair,
they root in the soil of my days, they are drunk with my heart's
   blood.

"Tear out of your hearts the dreadful beauty of flowers.
Walk your dark streets alone but without fear.
Go back to your death in life not caring to live or die,
and forget the crazy glance of the flowers out of a time gone by."

Birds

Whatever the bird is, is perfect in the bird.
Weapon kestrel hard as a blade's curve,
thrush round as a mother or a full drop of water,
fruit-green parrot wise in his shrieking swerve —
all are what bird is and do not reach beyond bird.

Whatever the bird does is right for the bird to do —
cruel kestrel dividing in his hunger the sky,
thrush in the trembling dew beginning to sing,
parrot clinging and quarrelling and veiling his queer eye —
all these are as birds are and good for birds to do.

But I am torn and beleaguered by my own people.
The blood that feeds my heart is the blood they gave me,
and my heart is the house where they gather and fight for
   dominion —
all different, all with a wish and a will to save me,
to turn me into the ways of other people.

If I could leave their battleground for the forest of a bird
I could melt the past, the present and the future in one
and find the words that lie behind all these languages.
Then I could fuse my passions into one clear stone
and be simple to myself as the bird is to the bird.

The Orange-Tree

The orange-tree that roots in night
draws from that night his great gold fruit,
and the green bough that stands upright
to shelter the bird with the beating heart.

Out of that silent death and cold
the tree leaps up and makes a world
to reconcile the night and day,
to feed the bird and the shining fly —

a perfect single world of gold
no storm can undo nor death deny.

Phaius Orchid

Out of the brackish sand
see the phaius orchid build
her intricate moonlight tower
that rusts away in flower.

For whose eyes — for whose eyes
does this blind being weave
sand's poverty, water's sour,
the white and black of the hour

into the image I hold
and cannot understand?
Is it for the ants, the bees,
the lizard outside his cave,

or is it to garland time —
eternity's cold tool
that severs with its blade
the gift as soon as made?

Then I too am your fool.
What can I do but believe?
Here like the plant I weave
your dying garlands, time.

Rain at Night

The wind from the desert over mountain and plain
gathered the loose unhappy dust
and set it running like a ghost from door to door again —
like the heart's red ghost
it ran to accuse me of the murder of the heart.
O little voice of the dry dust at the windowpane,
I wept for you before I slept
till in the night came on the undreamed-of rain.

Out of the seed of night and the divided dust
and the clouds of rain
what thrones are made, and stand up there in the east
to hold the sun!
What pure and shining altars rise in the night —
altars set with the ritual of love — the first
god that broke out when night's egg woke —
the blind and divine son of dust and night.
In the fierce rites of the flowers now, heart and heart's murderer
rest.

The Pool and the Star

Let me be most clear and most tender;
let no wind break my perfection.
Let the stream of my life run muted,
and a pure sleep unbar
my every depth and secret.

I wait for the rising of a star
whose spear of light shall transfix me —
of a far-off world whose silence
my very truth must answer.
That shaft shall pierce me through
till I cool its white-hot metal.

Let move no leaf nor moth;
sleep quietly, all my creatures.
I must be closed as the rose is
until that bright one rises.
Then down the fall of space
his kiss the shape of a star
shall wake the dark of my breast.

For this I am drawn from far —
for this I am gathered together.
Though made of time and of waters
that move even while I love
I shall draw from the living day
no hour as pure, as bright,
as this when across the night
he stoops with his steady ray
and his image burns on my breast.

All Things Conspire

All things conspire to hold me from you —
even my love,
since that would mask you and unname you
till merely woman and man we live.
All men wear arms against the rebel —
and they are wise,
since the sound world they know and stable
is eaten away by lovers' eyes.

All things conspire to stand between us —
even you and I,
who still command us, still unjoin us,
and drive us forward till we die.
Not till those fiery ghosts are laid
shall we be one.
Til then, they whet our double blade
and use the turning world for stone.

Our Love Is So Natural

Our love is so natural,
the wild animals move
gentle and light on
the shores of our love.

My eyes rest upon you,
to me your eyes turn,
as bee goes to honey,
as fire to fire will burn.

Bird and beast are at home,
and star lives in tree
when we are together
as we should be.

But so silent my heart falls
when you are away,
I can hear the world breathing
where he hides from our day.

My heart crouches under,
silent and still,
and the avalanche gathers
above the green hill.

Our love is so natural —
I cannot but fear.
I would reach out and touch you.
Why are you not here?

The Flame-Tree

How to live, I said, as the flame-tree lives?
— to know what the flame-tree knows; to be
prodigal of my life as that wild tree
and wear my passion so?
That lover's knot of water and earth and sun,
that easy answer to the question baffling reason,
branches out of my heart this sudden season.
I know what I would know.

How shall I thank you, who teach me how to wait
in quietness for the hour to ask or give:
to take and in taking bestow, in bestowing live:
in the loss of myself, to find?
This is the flame-tree; look how gloriously
that careless blossomer scatters, and more and more.
What the earth takes of her, it will restore.
These are the thanks of lovers who share one mind.   47

Song

When cries aloud the bird of night
then I am quiet on your breast.
When storms of darkness quench the trees
I turn to you and am at rest:
and when the ancient terrors rise
and the feet halt and grow unsure,
for each of us the other's eyes
restore the day, the sickness cure.

You, who with your insistent love
dissolved in me the evil stone
that was my shield against the world
and grew so close it seemed my own —
gave, easily as a tree might give
its fruit, its flower, its wild grey dove —
the very life by which I live;
the power to answer love with love.

Legend

The blacksmith's boy went out with a rifle
and a black dog running behind.
Cobwebs snatched at his feet,
rivers hindered him,
thorn-branches caught at his eyes to make him blind
and the sky turned into an unlucky opal,
but he didn't mind,
I can break branches, I can swim rivers, I can stare out any
    spider I meet,
said he to his dog and his rifle.

The blacksmith's boy went over the paddocks
with his old black hat on his head.
Mountains jumped in his way,

rocks rolled down on him,
and the old crow cried, "You'll soon be dead."
And the rain came down like mattocks.
But he only said
I can climb mountains, I can dodge rocks, I can shoot an old
  crow any day,
and he went on over the paddocks.

When he came to the end of the day the sun began falling.
Up came the night ready to swallow him,
like the barrel of a gun,
like an old black hat,
like a black dog hungry to follow him.
Then the pigeon, the magpie and the dove began wailing
and the grass lay down to pillow him.
His rifle broke, his hat blew away and his dog was gone
and the sun was falling.

But in front of the night the rainbow stood on the mountain,
just as his heart foretold.
He ran like a hare,
he climbed like a fox;
he caught it in his hands, the colours and the cold —
like a bar of ice, like the column of a fountain,
like a ring of gold.
The pigeon, the magpie and the dove flew up to stare,
and the grass stood up again on the mountain.

The blacksmith's boy hung the rainbow on his shoulder
instead of his broken gun.
Lizards ran out to see,
snakes made way for him,
and the rainbow shone as brightly as the sun.
All the world said, Nobody is braver, nobody is bolder,
nobody else has done
anything to equal it. He went home as bold as he could be
with the swinging rainbow on his shoulder.

Full Moon Rhyme

There's a hare in the moon tonight,
crouching alone in the bright
buttercup field of the moon;
and all the dogs in the world
howl at the hare in the moon.

"I chased that hare to the sky,"
the hungry dogs all cry.
"The hare jumped into the moon
and left me here in the cold.
I chased that hare to the moon."

"Come down again, mad hare,
we can see you there,"
the dogs all howl to the moon.
"Come down again to the world,
you mad black hare in the moon,

"or we will grow wings and fly
up to the star-grassed sky
to hunt you out of the moon,"
the hungry dogs of the world
howl at the hare in the moon.

To a Child

When I was a child I saw
a burning bird in a tree.
I see became *I am,*
I am became *I see.*

In winter dawns of frost
the lamp swung in my hand.
The battered moon on the slope
lay like a dune of sand;

and in the trap at my feet
the rabbit leapt and prayed,
weeping blood, and crouched
when the light shone on the blade.

The sudden sun lit up
the webs from wire to wire;
the white webs, the white dew,
blazed with a holy fire.

Flame of light in the dew,
flame of blood on the bush
answered the whirling sun
and the voice of the early thrush.

I think of this for you.
I would not have you believe
the world is empty of truth
or that men must grieve,

but hear the song of the martyrs
out of a bush of fire —
"All is consumed with love;
all is renewed with desire."

Drought

The summer solstice come and gone,
now the dark of the moon comes on.
The raging sun in his pale sky
has drunk the sap of the world dry.
Across the plains the dustwhirls run
and dust has choked the shrivelling tree.

This is my world that dies with me,
cries the curlew in the night.
I have forgotten how the white
birdfooted water in the creek

used in spring to call and speak.
All is fallen under the sun
and the world dies that once I made.

The strength that brandished my green blade,
the force uncoiling from the cell,
drains like water from a wrecked well,
says the dried corn out of the earth.
The seed I cherished finds no birth.

Now the dark of the world comes on.

Unknown Water

No rain yet, and the creek drying, and no rain coming;
and I remember the old man, part of my childhood,
who knew all about cattle and horses. In the big drought,
he said, the mares knew when their milk gave out,
and I've seen a mare over the dead foal
with tears coming out of her eyes. She kept on standing;
she wouldn't go near water or look for grass,
and when the rain came she stayed where the foal died,
though we dragged it away and burned it.

Old man, go easy with me.
The truth I am trying to tell is a kind of waterhole
never dried in any drought. You can understand that;
you lived by a water not like the cattle drank,
but the water you knew of is dried up now. All dried,
and the drought goes raging on. Your own sons and daughters
have forgotten what it is to live by a water
that never dries up. But I know of another creek.
You will not understand my words when I tell of it.

You do not understand me; yet you are part of me.
You understand the cattle and the horses
and knew the country you travelled in, and believed

what everyone believed when you were a child.
And I believed in you, and otherwise in nothing,
since the drought was coming, that dried up your waterholes;
and I still believe in you, though you will not understand me.

For the country I travelled through was not your kind of country;
and when I grew I lost the sound of your stories
and heard only at night in my dreams the sound of dogs
and cattle and galloping horses. I am not you,
but you are part of me. Go easy with me, old man;
I am helping to clear a track to unknown water.

The Lost Man

To reach the pool you must go through the rain-forest —
through the bewildering midsummer of darkness
lit with ancient fern,
laced with poison and thorn.
You must go by the way he went — the way of the bleeding
hand and feet, the blood on the stones like flowers,
under the hooded flowers
that fall on the stones like blood.

To reach the pool you must go by the black valley
among the crowding columns made of silence,
under the hanging clouds
of leaves and voiceless birds.
To go by the way he went to the voice of the water,
where the priest stinging-tree waits with his whips and fevers
under the hooded flowers
that fall from the trees like blood,

you must forget the song of the gold bird dancing
over tossed light; you must remember nothing
except the drag of darkness   *53*

that draws your weakness under.
To go by the way he went you must find beneath you
that last and faceless pool, and fall. And falling
find between breath and death
the sun by which you live.

FROM

The Two Fires

(1955)

The Two Fires

Among green shades and flowering ghosts, the remembrances of
  love,
inventions of the holy unwearying seed,
bright falling fountains made of time, that bore
through time the holy seed that knew no time —
I tell you, ghosts in the ghosts of summer days,
you are dead as though you never had been.
For time has caught on fire, and you too burn:
leaf, stem, branch, calyx and the bright corolla
are now the insubstantial wavering fire
in which love dies: the final pyre
of the beloved, the bridegroom and the bride.
These two we have denied.

In the beginning was the fire;
Out of the death of fire, rock and the waters;
and out of water and rock, the single spark, the divine truth.
Far, far below, the millions of rock-years divide
to make a place for those who were born and died
to build the house that held the bridegroom and the bride.
Those two, who reigned in passion in the flower,
whom still the hollow seasons celebrate,
no ritual now can recreate.
Whirled separate in the man-created fire

their cycles end, with the cycle of the holy seed;
the cycle from the first to the last fire.
These too time can divide;
these too have died.

And walking here among the dying centuries —
the centuries of moss, of fern, of cycad,
of the towering tree — the centuries of the flower —
I pause where water falls from the face of the rock.
My father rock, do you forget the kingdom of the fire?
The aeons grind you into bread —
into the soil that feeds the living and transforms the dead;
and have we eaten in the heart of the yellow wheat
the sullen unforgetting seed of fire?

And now, set free by the climate of man's hate,
that seeds sets time ablaze.
The leaves of fallen years, the forest of living days,
have caught like matchwood. Look, the whole world burns.
The ancient kingdom of the fire returns.
And the world, that flower that housed the bridegroom and the
     bride,
burns on the breast of night.
The world's denied.

Searchlight Practice

So simple the hour seems,
the night so clear;
if sight could teach us peace
we might learn here

to set ourselves aside,
to be alone,
to let the earth bear us
like a flower or a stone;

to let the hands fall,
the mind forget;
to move like trees in the wind;
to be the night.

Escape the angel? Escape
the bond, the curse?

Great swords in front of the stars
spring up and cross.

For the Loved
and the Unloved

Love in his alteration
invents the heart to suit him:
its season, spring or autumn,
depends on his decision.

The rose he sets his light in
increases by his brooding.
What colour the sepal's hiding
not even the tree is certain.

The bud bowed in and folded
round love's illumination
works by a light no vision
into our world has welded;

and nerve and artery follow
a track no mind is treading:
and what's the compass guiding
the far-returning swallow?

The roads unwind within us.
It is not time's undone us,
but we ourselves, who ravel
the thread by which we travel.

Dialogue

Above the child the cliffs of the years tower.
He dares not stop to play, he must climb higher.
The rotting ladders sway beneath his weight
and the winds rise and cry and storm comes nearer.
Oh passionate gazer, oh enraptured hearer,
oh eager climber, perhaps you climb too late.

Perhaps from the stone peak worn down and trodden
by worshipping generations, the view is hidden.
Nothing but thundering storm and blowing mist
will greet you; and the night will come to blind you
and the last ladder crumble and break behind you —
oh wait, my darling. The world you seek is lost.

Even if the cloud parted and in the dying
light of evening you saw that landscape lying,
you would see a paper map, a country of lost hopes;
seas scrawled by a million courses, ink-dried rivers,
and deserts littered with the bones of the world's lovers.
Turn back, my darling. Play for ever on these gentle slopes.

— "You do not know. You cannot hear the call,
nor see the face that leans from the cliff-wall.
You must not hold me, though you speak in kindness.
There waits, hidden beyond the known and charted,
World, the secret one, the flower-hearted —
her terrible innocence the measure of your blindness."

The Man Beneath the Tree

Nothing is so far as truth;
nothing is so plain to see.
Look where light has married earth
through the green leaves on the tree.

Nothing is so hard as love —
love for which the wisest weep;
yet the child who never looked
found it easily as his sleep.

Nothing is as strange as love —
love is like a foreign land.
Yet its natives find their way
natural as hand-in-hand.

Nothing is so bare as truth —
that lean geometry of thought;
but round its poles there congregate
all foliage, flowers and fruits of earth.

Oh, love and truth and I should meet,
sighed the man beneath the tree;
but where should our acquaintance be?
Between your hat and the soles of your feet,
sang the bird on top of the tree.

Cyclone and Aftermath

Hooded shadows out of a universe of weeping
crouch on the gale through the rack of trees; repetitive
of disaster, procession of fugitives. Vanishing
downhill each on the vanishing heel of the other
they form and are gone.
                    Nothing else visible
but the despair of trees against wind.
                    Navigators
wise to this coast are careful of these months,
but there is nothing that the tall rose-gums,
annually betrayed by summer's languors
into an overplus of leaves, can do about it.
Misfortune ruins their pride. They implore and gesture —
bent on the wheel, spring up in a moment's mercy

and with flung arms accuse her, betrayer, destroyer,
from whose inescapable injustice the hooded shadows fly.

Drenched flowers, bruised unripe fruit, limb wrenching the
    wound —
all that summer contrived of cunning ornament
tossed drowning, the old witch is furious still,
aiming and pelting water and air in unbreathable mixture,
till entity fades to ghost, labouring to hold a shape
against the universal wet — a shape that frays into water,
bruises into water at a touch, snaps at a pull.

This is her cruelty — that she has hung decay
like lace over the laughing brides of summer.
Fungus and mould spread their webs in the hush when the wind
    has fallen
and the tree fallen; the tall tree that meditated
dance after dance for white limbs crossing in winds
is dissolved in intent silence;
that lovely building debased, that tower pulled down.

This is her wisdom: she is not one thing nor the other.
Praise her if you like in the season of flower and serenity,
for it is hers: reproach her, oppressor of those
weeping swift-running shadows: it's she you are speaking of.
But look for her, too, when evening darkens and wind drops.
The shattered flowers melt into industrious earth;
the heron watches the pool, the high clouds stand
arena for the light's farewell. She is that figure
drawing the twilight's hood about her:
that wise woman from the land past joy or grief.

For Precision

Yet I go on from day to day, betraying
the core of light, the depth of darkness —
60   my speech inexact, the note not right,
never quite sure what I am saying —

on the periphery of truth. Uphold me now,
pure colours, blacks, whites, bells on the central tone,
middays, midnights. I wander among cross-lights.
Let me be sure and economical as the rayed
suns, stars, flowers, wheels: let me fall as a gull, a hawk

through the confusions of foggy talk,
and pin with one irremediable stroke —
what? — the escaping wavering wandering light,
the blur, the brilliance; forming into one chord
what's separate and distracted; making the vague hard —
catching the wraith — speaking with a pure voice,
and that the gull's sole note like a steel nail
that driven through cloud, sky, and irrelevant seas,
joins all, gives all a meaning, makes all whole.

Nameless Flower

Three white petals float
above the green.
You cannot think they spring from it
till the fine stem's seen.

So separated each from each,
and each so pure,
yet at the centre here they touch
and form a flower.

Flakes that drop at the flight of a bird
and have no name,
I'll set a word upon a word
to be your home.

Up from the dark and jungle floor
you have looked long.
Now I come to lock you here
in a white song.

Word and word are chosen and met.
Flower, come in.
But before the trap is set,
the prey is gone.

The words are white as a stone is white
carved for a grave;
but the flower blooms in immortal light,
Being now; being love.

Gum-Trees Stripping

Say the need's born within the tree,
and waits a trigger set for light;
say sap is tidal like the sea,
and rises with the solstice-heat —
but wisdom shells the words away
to watch this fountain slowed in air
where sun joins earth — to watch the place
at which these silent rituals are.

Words are not meanings for a tree.
So it is truer not to say,
"These rags look like humility,
or this year's wreck of last year's love,
or wounds ripped by the summer's claw."
If it is possible to be wise
here, wisdom lies outside the word
in the earlier answer of the eyes.

Wisdom can see the red, the rose,
the stained and sculptured curve of grey,
the charcoal scars of fire, and see
around that living tower of tree
the hermit tatters of old bark
split down and strip to end the season;
and can be quiet and not look
for reasons past the edge of reason.

From Seven Songs
from a Journey

III. Night

The contours of night are like
the contours of this rock,
and worn by light as by water.

The pin-sharp stars drag
their thin bright trails across it.
The moon's pale creek and the floods
of the sunlight erode it;
and round its secret flanks
the currents of the living —
plant, beast, man, and god —
swirl their phosphorescence.

Night is what remains
when the equation is finished.
Night is the earth's dream
that the sun is dead.
Night is man's dream
that he has invented God —
the dream of before-creation;
the dream of falling.

Night blocks our way, saying,
I at least am real.

The contours of night are like
the contours of this rock.

VI. Sea-Beach

Mountain, wall and tree
bear witness against our lives,
being scrawled with obsolete slogans —
initialled by clumsy knives:
No one has marked the sea.

Below high tide you can stand
as though you stood in the sky.
No sign on the clean sand
will stay to remember you by.

Sea, anonymous pilgrim
made free of time and place,
from the unhistoried poles
and the shores of Asia and Greece

you carry no memory,
you bear no symbol or gift,
except the unshaped bone,
the silver splinter of raft.

And though you beckon and play,
we will not stay here long.
We will snatch back the child
who trusts too far to your song.

The sea cleans everything,
a sailor said to me:
and these white empty shells
come out of the scour of the sea.

Sanctuary

The road beneath the giant original trees
sweeps on and cannot wait. Varnished by dew,
its darkness mimics mirrors and is bright
behind the panic eyes the driver sees
caught in headlights. Behind his wheels the night
takes over: only the road ahead is true.
It knows where it is going: we go too.

Sanctuary, the sign said. Sanctuary —
trees, not houses; flat skins pinned to the road
of possum and native cat; and here the old tree stood
for how many thousand years? — that old gnome-tree
some axe-new boy cut down. Sanctuary, it said:
but only the road has meaning here. It leads
into the world's cities like a long fuse laid.

Fuse, nerve, strand of a net, tense
bearer of messages, snap-tight violin-string,
dangerous knife-edge laid across the dark,
what has that sign to do with you? The immense
tower of antique forest and cliff, the rock
where years accumulate like leaves, the tree
where transient bird and mindless insect sing?
The word the board holds up is Sanctuary
and the road knows that notice-boards make sense

but has no time to pray. Only, up there,
morning sets doves upon the power-line.
Swung on that fatal voltage like a sign
and meaning love, perhaps they are a prayer.

At Cooloola

The blue crane fishing in Cooloola's twilight
has fished there longer than our centuries.
He is the certain heir of lake and evening,
and he will wear their colour till he dies,

but I'm a stranger, come of a conquering people.
I cannot share his calm, who watch his lake,
being unloved by all my eyes delight in,
and made uneasy, for an old murder's sake.

Those dark-skinned people who once named Cooloola
knew that no land is lost or won by wars,
for earth is spirit: the invader's feet will tangle
in nets there and his blood be thinned by fears.

Riding at noon and ninety years ago,
my grandfather was beckoned by a ghost —
a black accoutred warrior armed for fighting,
who sank into bare plain, as now into time past.

White shores of sand, plumed reed and paperbark,
clear heavenly levels frequented by crane and swan —
I know that we are justified only by love,
by oppressed by arrogant guilt, have room for none.

And walking on clean sand among the prints
of bird and animal, I am challenged by a driftwood spear
thrust from the water; and, like my grandfather,
must quiet a heart accused by its own fear.

Landscapes

To look at landscapes loved by the newly dead
is to move into the dark and out again.
Every brilliant leaf that lives by light
dies from its hold at last and desires earth's bed:
men and trees and grasses daily falling
make that veil of beauty for her. Slight
aeons of soil on rock, of grass on soil, of men
standing on grass, can't hide her outcrops. Stone —
stone our mother locks in, tongueless, without feeling,
our far blind brothers, future, and past who had no luck
and never was born. And now the newly dead
is lowered there. Now we weep for eyes whose look
is closed on landscapes loved, and at last known.

... and Mr Ferritt

But now Mr Ferritt
with his troublesome nose,
with his shaven chin
and his voice like a grief
that grates in dark corners,
moves in his house
and scrapes his dry skin
and sees it is morning.

O day, you sly thief,
now what have you taken
of all the small things
I tie on my life?
The radio serial
whines in the kitchen,
caught in a box,
and cannot get out.
The finch in his cage,
the border of phlox

as straight as a string
drawn up in my garden,
the potted geranium,
all are there.
But day from his cranium
twitches one hair;
and never again
will a hair grow there.
— O day, you sly thief,
how you pluck at my life,
frets Mr Ferritt;
but there, he must bear it.

Outside the fence
the wattle-tree grows.
It tosses; it shines;

it speaks its one word.
Beware, beware!
Mr Ferritt has heard.
— What are axes for?
What are fences for?
Who planted that wattle-tree
right at my door?
God only knows.
All over the garden
its dust is shaken.
No wonder I sneeze
as soon as I waken.

O world, you sly thief;
my youth you have taken,
and what have you given
who promised me heaven,
but a nagging wife
and a chronic catarrh,
and a blonde on the pictures
as far as a star?

And wild and gold
as a film-star's hair
that tree stands there,
blocking the view
from my twenty-perch block.
What are axes for,
what are fences for
but to keep this tree
away from my door?

And down came the tree.
But poor Mr Ferritt
still has hay-fever.
Nothing will cure it.

The Cup

Silence is harder, Una said.
If I could be quiet I might come true
like the blue cup hung over the sink,
which is not dead,
but waiting for someone to fill it and drink.

Una said, Silence can reach my mouth:
but a long way in my trouble lies.
The look in my eyes, the sound of my words
all tell the truth:
they spring from my trouble like a flight of birds.

Let silence travel, Una said,
by every track of nerve and vein
to heart and brain, where the troubles begin.
Then I shan't be dead,
but waiting for something to come in.

For a Birthday

(*to J. P. McK.*)

Bind — that word was spoken,
and there was I bound.
The rope can no more be broken
that then wrapped me round.

Live, I was commanded.
O life, your touch was strange.
There the flesh was founded
that bodies my change.

Act — my blood told me.
And so time began;
time, that now has filled me
with the whole world of man.

69

Love, from its unknown centre,
spins a silence like thought;
and deep there as the heart can enter
my wholeness I sought.

Decay; upon my body
that summons was served;
and now the flesh speaks sadly,
How can we be saved?

Build, though the world be falling,
that crystal, your truth.
Its eight sides shall be your dwelling
though time take your breath.

Request to a Year

If the year is meditating a suitable gift,
I should like it to be the attitude
of my great-great-grandmother,
legendary devotee of the arts,

who, having had eight children
and little opportunity for painting pictures,
sat one day on a high rock
beside a river in Switzerland

and from a difficult distance viewed
her second son, balanced on a small ice-floe,
drift down the current towards a waterfall
that struck rock-bottom eighty feet below,

while her second daughter, impeded,
no doubt, by the petticoats of the day,
stretched out a last-hope alpenstock
(which luckily later caught him on his way).

Nothing, it was evident, could be done;
and with the artist's isolating eye
my great-great-grandmother hastily sketched the scene.
The sketch survives to prove the story by.

Year, if you have no Mother's day present planned;
reach back and bring me the firmness of her hand.

Song

O where does the dancer dance —
the invisible centre spin —
whose bright periphery holds
the world we wander in?

For it is he we seek —
the source and death of desire;
we blind as blundering moths
around that heart of fire.

Caught between birth and death
we stand alone in the dark
to watch the blazing wheel
on which the earth is a spark,

crying, Where does the dancer dance —
the terrible centre spin,
whose flower will open at last
to let the wanderer in?

Wildflower Plain

The angry granite,
the hungry range,
must crumble away,

must melt and change;
forget the single
iron word
that no voice spoke
when no ear heard,
and learn this thorny,
delicate, tender
speech of the flower
as last surrender.
This various speech
that covers over
the gravel plain
like the words of a lover.

Blue orchid gentle
as skies seen early;
blown purple iris
so quick to wither;
tea-tree falling
on water-lily;
heath, boronia,
many another,
can but spring
where rock makes way.
Let rock be humble.
Let it decay.
Let time's old anger
become new earth,
to sign to the heart
the truth of death.

The Harp and the King

Old king without a throne,
the hollow of despair
behind his obstinate unyielding stare,

knows only, God is gone:
and, fingers clenching on his chair,
feels night and the soul's terror coming on.

Bring me that harp, that singer. Let him sing.
Let something fill the space inside the mind,
that's a dry stream-bed for the flood of fear.
Song's only sound; but it's a lovely sound,
a fountain through the drought. Bring David here,
said the old frightened king.

Sing something. Comfort me.
Make me believe the meaning in the rhyme.
The world's a traitor to the self-betrayed;
but once I thought there was a truth in time,
while now my terror is eternity.
So do not take me outside time.
Make me believe in my mortality,
since that is all I have, the old king said.

I sing the praise of time, the harp replied:
the time of aching drought when the black plain
cannot believe in roots or leaves or rain.
Then lips crack open in the stone-hard peaks;
and rock begins to suffer and to pray
when all that lives has died
and withered in the wind and blown away;
and earth has no more strength to bleed.

I sing the praise of time and of the rain —
the word creation speaks.
Four elements are locked in time;
the sign that makes them fertile is the seed,
and this outlasts all death and springs again,
the running water of the harp-notes cried.

But the old king sighed obstinately,
How can that comfort me?
Night and the terror of the soul come on,
and out of me both water and seed have gone.

What other generations shall I see?
But make me trust my failure and my fall,
said the sad king, since these are now my all.

I sing the praise of time, the harp replied.
In time we fail, alone with hours and tears,
ruin our followers and traduce our cause,
and give our love its last and fatal hurt.
In time we fail and fall.
In time the company even of God withdraws
and we are left with our own murderous heart.

Yet it is time that holds,
somewhere although not now,
the peal of trumpets for us; time that bears,
made fertile even by those tears,
even by this darkness, even by this loss,
incredible redemptions — hours that grow,
as trees grow fruit, in a blind holiness,
the truths unknown, the loves unloved by us.

But the old king turned his head sullenly.
How can that comfort me,
who sees into the heart as deep as God can see?
Love's sown in us; perhaps it flowers; it dies.
I failed my God and I betrayed my love.
Make me believe in treason; that is all I have.

This is the praise of time, the harp cried out —
that we betray all truths that we possess.
Time strips the soul and leaves it comfortless
and sends it thristy through a bone-white drought.
Time's subtler treacheries teach us to betray.
What else could drive us on our way?
Wounded we cross the desert's emptiness,
and must be false to what would make us whole.
For only change and distance shape for us
some new tremendous symbol for the soul.

Birds

(1962)

The Peacock

Shame on the aldermen who locked
the Peacock in a dirty cage!
His blue and copper sheens are mocked
by habit, hopelessness and age.

The weary Sunday families
along their gravelled paths repeat
the pattern of monotonies
that he treads out with restless feet.

And yet the Peacock shines alone;
and if one metal feather fall
another grows where that was grown.
Love clothes him still, in spite of all.

How pure the hidden spring must rise
that time and custom cannot stain!
It speaks its joy again — again.
Perhaps the aldermen are wise.

Winter Kestrel

Fierce with hunger and cold
all night in the windy tree
the kestrel to the sun cries,
"Oh bird in the egg of the sea,

"break out, and tower, and hang
high, oh most high,
and watch for the running mouse
with your unwearying eye;

"and I shall hover and hunt,
and I shall see him move,
and I like a bolt of power
shall seize him from above.

"Break from your blue shell,
you burning Bird or God,
and light me to my kill —
and you shall share his blood."

Egrets

Once as I travelled through a quiet evening,
I saw a pool, jet-black and mirror-still.
Beyond, the slender paperbarks stood crowding;
each on its own white image looked its fill,
and nothing moved but thirty egrets wading —
thirty egrets in a quiet evening.

Once in a lifetime, lovely past believing,
your lucky eyes may light on such a pool.
As though for many years I had been waiting,
I watched in silence, till my heart was full
of clear dark water, and white trees unmoving,
and, whiter yet, those thirty egrets wading.

"Dove—Love"

The dove purrs — over and over the dove
purrs its declaration. The wind's tone
changes from tree to tree, the creek on stone
alters its sob and fall, but still the dove
goes insistently on, telling its love
      "I could eat you."

And in captivity, they say, doves do.
Gentle, methodical, starting with the feet
(the ham-pink succulent toes
on their thin stems of rose),
baring feather by feather the wincing meat:
      "I could eat you."

That neat suburban head, that suit of grey,
watchful conventional eye and manicured claw —
these also rhyme with us. The doves play
on one repetitive note that plucks the raw
helpless nerve, their soft "I do. I do.
      I could eat you."

Migrant Swift

Beneath him slid the furrows of the sea;
against his sickle-skill the air divided;
he used its thrust and current easily.

He trusted all to air: the flesh that bred him
was worn against it to a blade-thin curving
made all for flight; air's very creatures fed him.

Such pride as this, once fallen, there's no saving.
Whatever struck him snapped his stretch of wing.
He came to earth at last, Icarus diving.

Like a contraption of feathers, bone and string,
his storm-blue wings hung useless. Yet his eyes
lived in his wreckage — head still strove to rise
and turn towards the lost impossible spring.

Apostle-Birds

Strangers are easily put out of countenance,
and we were strangers in that place;
camped among trees we had no names for;
not knowing the local customs.

And those big grey birds, how they talked about us!
They hung head-down from branches and peered.
They spread their tawny wings like fans,
and came so close we could have touched them;
staring with blunt amusement.
It was ridiculous to feel embarrassed.

Of that camp I remember the large wild violets,
the sound of the creek on stones,
the wind-combed grass, the tree-trunks
wrinkled and grey like elephant-legs all round us;
and those apostle-birds, so rude to strangers,
so self-possessed and clannish,
we were glad when they flew away.

Magpies

Along the road the magpies walk
with hands in pockets, left and right.
They tilt their heads, and stroll and talk.
In their well-fitted black and white

they look like certain gentlemen
who seem most nonchalant and wise
until their meal is served — and then
what clashing beaks, what greedy eyes!

But not one man that I have heard
throws back his head in such a song
of grace and praise — no man nor bird.
Their greed is brief; their joy is long,
for each is born with such a throat
as thanks his God with every note.

Wounded Night-Bird

Walking one lukewarm, lamp-black night I heard
a yard from me his harsh rattle of warning,
and in a landing-net of torchlight saw him crouch —
the devil, small but dangerous. My heart's lurch
betrayed me to myself. But I am learning:
I can distinguish: the devil is no bird.

A bird with a broken breast. But what a stare
he fronted me with! — his look abashed my own.
He was all eyes, furious, meant to wound.
And I, who meant to heal, took in my hand
his depth of down, his air-light delicate bone,
his heart in the last extreme of pain and fear.

From nerve to nerve I felt the circuit blaze.
Along my veins his anguish beat; his eyes
flared terror into mine and cancelled time,
and the black whirlpool closed over my head
and clogged my throat with the cry that knows no aid.
Far down beneath the reach of succouring light
we fought, we suffered, we were sunk in night.

Pelicans

Funnel-web spider, snake and octopus,
pitcher-plant and vampire-bat and shark —
these are cold water on an easy faith.
Look at them, but don't linger.
If we stare too long, something looks back at us;
something gazes through from underneath;
something crooks a very dreadful finger
down there in an unforgotten dark.

Turn away then, and look up at the sky.
There sails that old clever Noah's Ark,
the well-turned, well-carved pelican
with his wise comic eye;
he turns and wheels down, kind as an ambulance-driver,
to join his fleet. Pelicans rock together,
solemn as clowns in white on a circus-river,
meaning: this world holds every sort of weather.

Silver Terns

It was a morning blue as ocean's mirror,
and strong and warm the wind was blowing.
Along the shore a flock of terns went flying,
their long white wings as clean as pearl.

Inland among the boulders of grey coral
their mates upon the eggs sat waiting.
A shoal of fishes hurried by the island
and the terns plunged into the shoal.

The sea was pocked with sudden silver fountains
where the birds dived, so swift and clever;
and some rose with a flash of fish and water
as sunlight broke on splash and scale;

but some, we saw, stayed down and did not rise.
That shoal the big bonito harried,
and they took fish and diving bird together.
One tern rose like a bloodied sail,

and a bonito leapt to make its capture.
All morning it went on, that slaughter,
with white birds diving, obstinate with hunger;
and some would rise, and some would fail.

The morning was as gentle as a pearl,
the sea was pocked with sudden silver fountains;
you would not guess the blood, unless you saw it,
that the waves washed from feather and from scale.

Black Swans

Night after night the rounding moon
rose like a bushfire through the air.
Night after night the swans came in —
the lake at morning rocked them there.

The inland fired the western wind
from plains bared by a year-long drought.
Only the coastal lakes were kind
until that bitter year ran out.

Black swans shadowed the blaze of moon
as they came curving down the sky.
On hills of night the red stars burned
like sparks blown where the wind is high.
On rushing wings the black swans turned
sounding aloud their desolate cry.

Lyrebirds

Over the west side of this mountain,
that's lyrebird country.
I could go down there, they say, in the early morning,
and I'd see them, I'd hear them.

Ten years, and I have never gone.
I'll never go.
I'll never see the lyrebirds —
the few, the shy, the fabulous,
the dying poets.

I should see them, if I lay there in the dew:
first a single movement
like a waterdrop falling, then stillness,
then a brown head, brown eyes,
a splendid bird, bearing
like a crest the symbol of his art,
the high symmetrical shape of the perfect lyre.
I should hear that master practising his art.

No, I have never gone.
Some things ought to be left secret, alone;
some things — birds like walking fables —
ought to inhabit nowhere but the reverence of the heart.

Brush Turkey

Right to the edge of his forest
the tourists come.
He learns the scavenger's habits
with scrap and crumb —
his forests shrunk, he lives
on what the moment gives:
pretends, in mockery,
to beg our charity.

Cunning and shy one must be
to snatch one's bread
from oafs whose hands are quicker
with stones instead.
He apes the backyard bird,
half proud and half absurd,
sheltered by his quick wit,
he sees and takes his bit.

Ash-black, wattles of scarlet,
and careful eye,
he hoaxes the ape, the ogre,
with mimicry.
Scornfully, he will eat
thrown crust and broken meat
till suddenly — "See, oh see!
The turkey's in the tree."

The backyard bird is stupid;
he trusts and takes.
But this one's wiles are wary
to guard against the axe:
escaping, neat and pat,
into his habitat.
Charred log and shade and stone
accept him. He is gone.

And here's a bird the poet
may ponder over,
whose ancient forest-meanings
no longer grant him cover;
who, circumspect yet proud,
like yet unlike the crowd,
must cheat its chucklehead
to throw — not stones, but bread.

The Koel

One spring when life itself was happiness,
he called and called across the orange-trees
his two strange syllables; and clouds of perfume
followed along the hesitating breeze.

And when he calls, the spring has come again,
and the old joy floods up in memory.
Yet his sad foster-kin cannot forget
the wrong he does them — Cain from his infancy.

Dark wary rebel, migrant without a home
except the spring, bird whom so many hate,
voice of one tune and only one — yet come.
In fear yet boldly, come and find your mate.
Against their anger, outcast by them all,
choose your one love and call your single call —
the endless tale you cannot cease to tell,
half-question, half-reply — *Koel! Koel!*

Extinct Birds

Charles Harpur in his journals long ago
(written in hope and love, and never printed)
recorded the birds of his time's forest —
birds long vanished with the fallen forest —
described in copperplate on unread pages.

The scarlet satin-bird, swung like a lamp in berries,
he watched in love, and then in hope described it.
There was a bird, blue, small, spangled like dew.
All now are vanished with the fallen forest.
And he, unloved, past hope, was buried,

who helped with proud stained hands to fell the forest,
and set those birds in love on unread pages;
yet thought himself immortal, being a poet.
And is he not immortal, where I found him,
in love and hope along his careful pages? —
the poet vanished, in the vanished forest,
among his brightly tinted extinct birds?

Dotterel

Wild and impermanent
as the sea-foam blown,
the dotterel keeps its distance
and runs alone.

Bare beach, salt wind,
its loved solitude,
hold all that it asks
of shelter and food.

I saw its single egg
dropped on the sand,
with neither straw nor wall
to warm or defend;

and the new-hatched chick,
like a thistle's pale down,
fled and crouched quiet
as sand or as stone.

Water's edge, land's edge
and edge of the air —
the dotterel chooses
to live nowhere.

It runs, but not in fear,
and its thin high call
is like a far bugle
that troubles the soul.

Fives Senses (The Forest)

(1963)

The Beasts

The wolf's desires pace through his cage
and try the long-neglected bars.
There is a meaning in his eyes,
a knowledge in his rage.

A life withheld by iron and stone
stays perfect in the lion's skin.
Nightmares have night to plunder in
and make their message known.

Therefore the wolf and lion rise
to prey upon my sighing sleep.
There is a purpose in their eyes
and in the tears I weep.

Their famine's ambush waits to kill
within my heart's dark hinterland.
It is my unlaid fear until
I take love's food in either hand,

and travel searching through the wild
till beast and man are reconciled.

The Forest

When first I knew this forest
its flowers were strange.
Their different forms and faces
changed with the seasons' change —

white violets smudged with purple,
the wild-ginger spray,
ground-orchids small and single
haunted my day;

the thick-fleshed Murray-lily,
flame-tree's bright blood,
and where the creek runs shallow,
the cunjevoi's green hood.

When first I knew this forest,
time was to spend,
and time's renewing harvest
could never reach an end.

Now that its vines and flowers
are named and known,
like long-fulfilled desires
those first strange joys are gone.

My search is further.
There's still to name and know
beyond the flowers I gather
that one that does not wither —
the truth from which they grow.

Five Senses

Now my five senses
gather into a meaning
all acts, all presences;
and as a lily gathers
the elements together,
in me this dark and shining,
that stillness and that moving,
these shapes that spring from nothing,
become a rhythm that dances,
a pure design.

While I'm in my five senses
they send me spinning
all sounds and silences,
all shape and colour
as thread for that weaver,
whose web within me growing
follows beyond my knowing
some pattern sprung from nothing —
a rhythm that dances
and is not mine.

The Nautilus

Some queer unshaped uncoloured animal,
much like a moment's pause of smoke or mist,
was yet so made that nothing less
than this hard perfect shape involving it
would do to speak its meaning in the world.

Out of its birth it came with this.
The smallest spiral holds the history
of something tiny in the battering sea,
that carried on its obstinate gathering,

89

till the years swelled in it to one last perfect
ballooning curve of colour laid by colour.
All was implicit in its hold on time.

Say that the thing was slave to its own meaning
and the unconscious labour of its body.
The terms were these, that it could never guess
how it conspired with time to shroud itself —
a splendid action common to its kind
but never known in doing.

Not even the end of making gave the meaning.
The thing it made was its own self, enclosed it,
and was the prison that prevented sight.
Yet though death strands its emptied spiral,
this sweet completion puts a term to time;
and that, I take it, was the bargain.

The Lake

All day the candid staring of the lake
holds what's passing and forgets the past.
Faithful to cloud and leaf, not knowing leaf nor cloud,
it spreads its smooth eye wide for something's sake.
All daylight's there; and all the night at last
drops threads of light from star to under-star.

Eye of the earth, my meaning's what you are.
You see no tree nor cloud. That's what I take
out of your waters in this net I cast —
the net where time is knotted by the word,
that flying needle. Lakes and eyes at last
drain dry, but the net-maker still must make.

What lover's shuttle flew when all began?
Who chose the images this net can draw? —
sun, moon and cloud, the hanging leaves and trees,

and leaning through, the terrible face of man:
my face. I looked, and there my eyes met eyes,
lover to lover. Deep I looked, and saw.

Interplay

What is within becomes what is around.
This angel morning on the world-wild sea
is seared with light that's mine and comes from me,
and I am mirror to its blaze and sound,
as lovers double in their interchange.

Yet I am not the seer, nor world the sight;
I am transcended by a single word —
Let there be light — and all creation stirred.
I am that cry alone, that visioned light,
its voice and focus. It's the word that's strange.

Look how the stars' bright chaos eddies in
to form our constellations. Flame by flame
answers the ordering image in the name.
World's signed with words; there light — there love begin.

Old Woman's Song

The moon drained white by day
lifts from the hill
where the old pear-tree, fallen in storm,
puts out some blossom still.

Women believe in the moon.
This branch I hold
is not more white and still than she
whose flower is ages old;

and so I carry home
this branch of pear
that makes such obstinate tokens still
of fruit it cannot bear.

Age to Youth

The sooty bush in the park
is green as any forest
for the boy to lie beneath,
with his arms around his dearest;

the black of the back street
is washed as any cloud
when the girl and the boy
touch hands among the crowd.

No, nothing's better than love,
than to want and to hold:
it is wise in the young
to forget the common world:

to be lost in the flesh
and the light shining there:
not to listen to the old
whose tune is fear and care —

who tell them love's a drink
poisoned with sorrow,
the flesh a flower today
and withered by tomorrow.

It is wise in the young
to let heart go racing heart,
to believe that the earth
is young and safe and sweet;

and the message we should send
from age back to youth
is that every kiss and glance
is truer than the truth;

that whatever we repent
of the time that we live,
it is never what we give —
it is never that we love.

Double Image

The long-dead living forest rose
as white as bone, as dark as hair.
In rage the old protagonists
fought for my life; and I was there.

My kinsman's flesh, my kinsman's skull
enclosed me, and our wounds were one.
The long-dead forest reeled and sank
before that bitter night was done —

before we struck and tore again
the jumping flesh from out his hide,
and drank the blood that ran and slowed
to show the moment when he died.

O curve of horror in the claw,
and speech within the speechless eye —
when one must die, not knowing death,
and one knows death who cannot die.

They run from me, my child, my love,
when in those long-dead forests caught
I pace. My tears behind his eyes,
my kinsman dreams of what is not —

dreaming of knowledge and of love
in agony he treads his path.
I bud in him, a thorn, a pain,
and yet my nightmare holds us both.

I drink his murder's choking blood,
and he in ignorance sheds my tears.
The centuries bind us each in each —
the tongueless word, the ignorant ears.

Till from those centuries I wake,
naked and howling, still unmade,
within the forests of my heart
my dangerous kinsman runs afraid.

Judas in Modern Dress

Not like those men they tell of, who just as suddenly
walk out of life, from wife and fire and cooking-pot
and the whole confusion, to sit alone and naked
and move past motion; gaze through dark and day
with eyes that answer neither. Having completed their journey
they are free to travel past the end of journeys.
But I stepped out alone.
"I reject the journey; it was not I who chose it.
I worked for one end only,
to find the key that lets me through the door
marked Exit. I have found it and I use it."

There is a tale I heard a wise man tell,
how, tattered with age, beneath a fruiting tree
a seeker sat, and heard in God's great silence
another traveller, caught in the nets of self,
weeping between anguish and ecstasy,
and over a thousand miles stretched out one hand
to pluck him back again into the Way.

But I was one the saints knew not at all.
A mocking man, a sad man-animal
rejecting world and sense
not for God's love, but man's intelligence;
as though a hog looked through a human eye
and saw the human world as dunged as its own sty,
foul ante-room to death. Like that I saw
the abattoir ahead, and smelt the soil
soaked under me with blood. No place for me.

And wise in my own way I worked to find
the weak place in the palings of the Real —
the gap between the Word
and its Creation, the act and the conception —
and forced my way between those married two,
set time against eternity, struggled through,
slipped through annihilation, still being I.

What violence those great powers did to me
as I escaped between, I have forgotten.
But swinging clear I saw the world spin by
and leave me, empty as an insect-shell,
beyond the chance of death, and outside time.

I had the choice. Once I had infinite choices —
all the variety of light and shadow
that sprang to being when Choice first was made.
Now I have knowledge only. Knowledge, and eyes
to watch the worlds cross their eternities.

Times after times the saving word is spoken.
Times after times I feel it wither me.
The fools of time live on and never hear,
and I who hear have chosen not to answer.
It beats against me till my ears are broken.

Times after times I see my death go by
and cannot reach it even with a prayer.
Indeed, since I am neither Here nor There
I cannot live, and therefore cannot die.

Times after times my lips begin to form
the word that I renounced, and close again.
The worlds pass jostling, and their makers dream
immortal life betrayed to daily pain —
the pain that I denied.

I still deny it.

O sweet, sweet, sweet the love in human eyes —
the tree of blossom dressed to meet the bee,
all white, all radiant, golden at the heart.
Halt there, at your Creation! And it dies,
dies into rotting fruit, and tyrannous seed.
If it spring up again, so much the worse.
That was the curse on Eden, Adam's curse.
The curse by which my heart will not abide.

If I am Judas, still my cause is good.
I will not move my lips to answer God.

Reason and Unreason

When I began to test my heart,
its laws and fantasies, against the world,
the pain of impact made me sad.
Where heart was curved the world ran straight,
where it lay warm the world came cold.
It seemed my heart, or else the world, was mad.

Could I reject arithmetics,
their plain unanswerable arguings,
or find a cranny outside categories,
where two and two made soldiers, love or six?
My heart observed the silence round its songs,
the indifference that met its stories;

believed itself a changeling crazed,
and bowed its head to every claim of reason;
but then stood up and realized
when work is over love begins its season;
each day is contraried by night
and Caesar's coin is paid for Venus' rite;

and knew its fantasies, since time began,
outdone by earth's wild dreams, Plant, Beast and Man.

For My Daughter

The days begin to set
your difference in your face.
The world has caught you up
to go at the world's pace.
Time, that is not denied,
as once from my heart it drew
the blood that nourished you,
now draws you from my side.

My body gave you then
what was ordained to give,
and did not need my will.
But now we learn to live
apart, what must I do?
Out of my poverty
what new gift can there be
that I can find for you?

Love was our first exchange —
the kindness of the blood.
Animals know as much,
and know that it is good.
But when the child is grown

and the mouth leaves the breast,
such simple good is past
and leaves us more alone.

So we grow separate
and separate spend our days.
You must become your world
and follow in its ways;
but out of my own need,
not knowing where nor how,
I too must journey now
upon a different road.

While love is innocent
the lion walks beside.
But when the spell's undone
and where the paths divide,
he must be tamed, or slain,
or else the heart's undone.
The path I walk upon
leads to his den again.

When I shall meet with him
I pray to wrestle well;
I pray to learn the way
to tame him, not to kill.
Then he may be my friend,
as Una's once, in love,
and I shall understand
what gifts are mine to give.

Naming the Stars

Now all the garden's overcome with dark,
its flowers transplanted, low to high,
become night's far-off suns, and map in hand
we find where Sirius and Canopus stand

and trace our birth-stars on the zodiac.
Is it not strange that you and I
should write those names like jewels on the sky?

My Twins shine in the north, your red-eyed Bull
runs at Orion, each horn ablaze;
but who are we to claim them? Far and far
they fly, and no star sees his brother star;
not Castor knows his twin among them all,
and Taurus with his Pleiades
is the old figure of a dead man's gaze.

Yet they, like us, are caught in time and cause
and eddied on their single stream.
Earth watches through our eyes, and as we stare
she greets, by us, her far compatriots there,
the wildhaired Suns and the calm Wanderers.
Her ancient thought is marked in every name;
hero and creature mingle in her dream.

On her dark breast we spring like points of light
and set her language on the map of night.

The Diver

The diver pausing on the tower
draws in one breath —
the crest of time, the pride, the hour
that answers death —
and down to where the long pool lies
marks out his curve;
descending light that star-like flies
from air to wave
as summer falls from trees and eyes,
and youth, and love.

Then from the rocking depths' release,
naked and new
the headfirst man springs up, and sees
all still to do —
the tower to climb, the pause to make,
the fill of breath
to gather in — the step to take
from birth to death.

Then, you who turn and climb the stair
and stand alone —
with you I draw that breath, and dare,
time's worst being known.

Reading Thomas Traherne

Can I then lose myself,
and losing find one word
that, in the face of what you were,
needs to be said or heard?

— Or speak of what has come
to your sad race
that to your clear rejoicing
we turn with such a face?

With such a face, Traherne,
as might make dumb
any but you, the man who knew
how simply truth may come:

who saw the depth of darkness
shake, part and move,
and from death's centre the light's ladder
go up from love to Love.

Autumn Fires

Old flower-stems turn to sticks in autumn,
clutter the garden, need
the discipline of secateurs.
Choked overplus, straggle of weed,
could souring strangling webs of root;

I pile the barrow with the lot.
Snapped twig that forgets flower and fruit,
thornbranch too hard to rot,
I stack you high for a last rite.

When twigs are built and match is set,
your death springs up like life; its flare
crowns and consumes the ended year.
Corruption changes to desire
that sears the pure and wavering air,
and death goes upward like a prayer.

The Other Half

(1966)

The Other Half

The self that night undrowns when I'm asleep
travels beneath the dumb days that I give,
within the limits set that I may live,
and beats in anger on the things I love.
I am the cross it bears, and it the tears I weep.

Under the eyes of light my work is brief.
Day sets on me the burdens that I carry.
I face the light, the dark of me I bury.
My silent answer and my other half,
we meet at midnight and by music only.

Yet there's a word that I would give to you:
the truth you tell in your dumb images
my daylight self goes stumbling after too.
So we may meet at last, and meeting bless,
and turn into one truth in singleness.

To Hafiz of Shiraz

The rose has come into the garden, from
Nothingness into Being.

Once I did not know the birds were described,
classified, observed, fixed in their proper localities.
Each bird that sprang from its tree, passed overhead, hawked
    from the bough,
was sole, new, dressed as no other was dressed.
Any leaf might hide the paradise-bird.

Once I believed any poem might follow my pen,
any road might beckon my feet to mapless horizons,
any eyes that I met, any hand that I took, any word that I heard
might pierce to my heart, stay forever in mine, open worlds on
    its hinge.
All then seemed possible; time and world were my own.

Now that I know that each star has its path, each bird
is finally feathered and grown in the unbroken shell,
each tree in the seed, each song in the life laid down —
is the night sky any less strange; should my glance less follow
    the flight;
should the pen shake less in my hand?

No, more and more like a birth looks the scheduled rising of
    Venus:
the turn of a wing in the wind more startles my blood.
Every path and life leads one way only,
out of continual miracle, through creation's fable,
over and over repeated but never yet understood,
as every word leads back to the blinding original Word.

To Another Housewife

Do you remember how we went,
on duty bound, to feed the crowd
of hungry dogs your father kept
as rabbit-hunters? Lean and loud,
half-starved and furious, how they leapt
against their chains, as though they meant
in mindless rage for being fed,
to tear our childish hands instead!

With tomahawk and knife we hacked
the flyblown tatters of old meat,
gagged at their carcass-smell, and threw
the scraps and watched the hungry eat.
Then turning faint, we made a pact,
(two greensick girls), crossed hearts and swore
to touch no meat forever more.

How many cuts of choice and prime
our housewife hands have dressed since then —
these hands with love and blood imbrued —
for daughters, sons, and hungry men!
How many creatures bred for food
we've raised and fattened for the time
they met at last the steaming knife
that serves the feast of death-in-life!

And as the evening meal is served
we hear the turned-down radio
begin to tell the evening news
just as the family joint is carved.
O murder, famine, pious wars . . .
Our children shrink to see us so,
in sudden meditation, stand
with knife and fork in either hand.

Wishes

What would I wish to be?
I wish to be wise.
From the swamps of fear and greed
free me and let me rise.
There was a poet once
spoke clear as a well-cast bell.
Rumí his name; his voice
rings perfect still.
O could I make one verse
but half so well!

What do I wish to do?
I wish to love:
that verb at whose source all verbs
take fire and learn to move.
Yes, could I rightly love,
all action, all event,
would from my nature spring
true as creation meant.
Love takes no pains with words
but is most eloquent.

To love, and to be wise?
Down, fool, and lower your eyes.

The Real Dream

There is intellectual pride in the silence of contemplation.
I have called myself poet, extracted from life its images,
then found myself silenced by that great rock in my way —
the silence before and after me: the oblation
that prefigures my sacrifice; the human and animal visages
that enact their poetry, reflect their night and day.

So one night I sat and wrote of imagined death
while on the black road outside, beyond my knowing,
some small crushed creature suffered a real end,
discovered in fading eyes the slow withdrawal of breath,
the blood leaving the veins, the warmth going,
and all the bent sky meant and could not amend.

And so out of a real dream dreamed below my will
I have woken and felt on my cheek the touch of cold
blown on a wind from a southern plain of ice
untouched, uninhabited. Images known can kill;
and in my warm bed I prayed my way over that field
taking no joy in silence, no pride in that image
of — oh my courted one — your terrible contemplation.

Homecoming

Spring, and the road is plushed with tender dust;
the house waits near and is expecting him.
Its elm puts on a glory, lit yet dim
with mingled light and leaf; there is a thrust
of irresistible budding. On the road
he walks, head up, just balancing its load;

the scarcely bearable load of bitter self
clamped firm, accepted closer day by day
since he stepped out of doors and went away.
Now, rooms made ready, flowers posed on the shelf,
linen ironed white, joy tremblingly arrayed,
you find yourselves made foolish and betrayed.

Take off your tenderness; let the petals fall.
Only one thing here he will recognize:
behind the glowing elm, the nesting cries
of garden birds, as grey, as stern and tall
as in his childhood, the steel pylon stands
gripping its deadly message in cold hands.

Brother, we dare not fail our load. Now brace
your skeleton's height, and hold. Danger and power
is ours; control and measure. Did we flower
our flowers would kill: but that is not our place.
Winter's perpetual gale we know, no more.
Shoulder the weight. Stride on. Open the door.

Cleaning Day

I carried rubbish down
until the house was clean,
cupboards scoured, shelves ransacked and bare.
High the heap grew;
I struck the match and blew
while the flame sulked against the idle air.

Sheltered, coaxed and fed,
slowly it caught and spread
till I could stand and watch its upward stream —
the gesture, the intent
spiralling, violent
dance that began around the core of flame.

Humble and worn-out things
put up their scarlet wings.
To new and pure sprang up the grey and old;
until a self-made wind
eddied within my mind
and drew it upward in a heat of gold.

O fire the poets I know,
I kneel, I strike, I blow.

Eve to Her Daughters

It was not I who began it.
Turned out into draughty caves,
hungry so often, having to work for our bread,
hearing the children whining,
I was nevertheless not unhappy.
Where Adam went I was fairly contented to go.
I adapted myself to the punishment: it was my life.

But Adam, you know . . . !
He kept on brooding over the insult,
over the trick They had played on us, over the scolding.
He had discovered a flaw in himself
and he had to make up for it.

Outside Eden the earth was imperfect,
the seasons changed, the game was fleet-footed,
he had to work for our living, and he didn't like it.
He even complained of my cooking
(it was hard to compete with Heaven).

So he set to work.
The earth must be made a new Eden
with central heating, domesticated animals,
mechanical harvesters, combustion engines,
escalators, refrigerators,
and modern means of communication
and multiplied opportunities for safe investment
and higher education for Abel and Cain
and the rest of the family.
You can see how his pride had been hurt.

In the process he had to unravel everything,
because he believed that mechanism
was the whole secret — he was always mechanical-minded.
He got to the very inside of the whole machine
exclaiming as he went, So this is how it works!

And now that I know how it works, why, I must have invented
    it.
As for God and the Other, they cannot be demonstrated,
and what cannot be demonstrated
doesn't exist.
You see, he had always been jealous.

Yes, he got to the centre
where nothing at all can be demonstrated.
And clearly he doesn't exist; but he refuses
to accept the conclusion.
You see, he was always an egotist.

It was warmer than this in the cave;
there was none of this fall-out.
I would suggest, for the sake of the children,
that it's time you took over.

But you are my daughters, you inherit my own faults of
    character;
you are submissive, following Adam
even beyond existence.
Faults of character have their own logic
and it always works out.
I observed this with Abel and Cain.

Perhaps the whole elaborate fable
right from the beginning
is meant to demonstrate this; perhaps it's the whole secret.
Perhaps nothing exists but our faults?
At least they can be demonstrated.

But it's useless to make
such a suggestion to Adam.
He has turned himself into God,
who is faultless, and doesn't exist.

Remembering an Aunt

Her room was large enough — you would say, private
from the rest of the house, until you looked again
and saw it supervised by her mother's window.
She kept there, face to the wall, some of the pictures
she had once painted; in a cupboard she had carved
was closed some music she had wished to play.

Her hands were pricked and blackened. At the piano
she played the pieces her mother liked to hear —
Chopin and Chaminade, In a Persian Market.
Her smile was awkward. When they said to her,
"Why not take up your sketching again? So pretty — "
she was abrupt. For she remembered Rome,
Florence, the galleries she saw at thirty,
she who had won art prizes at local shows
and played to country women from her childhood.

Brushes, paints, Beethoven put aside
(for ignorant flattery's worse than ignorant blame),
she took her stance and held it till she died.

I praise her for her silence and her pride;
art lay in both. Yet in her, all the same,
sometimes there sprang a small unnoticed flame —
grief too unseen, resentment too denied.

Typists in the Phoenix Building

In tiled and fireproof corridors
the typists shelter in their sex;
perking beside the half-cock clerks
they set a curl on freckled necks.
The formal bird above the doors

is set in metal whorls of flame.
The train goes aching on its rails.
Its rising cry of steel and wheels
intolerably comes, and fails
on walls immaculate and dumb.

Comptometers and calculators
compute the frequency of fires,
adduce the risk, add up the years.
Drawn by late-afternoon desires
the poles of mind meet lust's equators.

Where will the inundation reach
whose cycle we can but await?
The city burns in summer's heat,
grass withers and the season's late;
the metal bird would scorch the touch;

and yet above some distant source,
some shrunken lake or spring gone dry,
perhaps the clouds involve the day
in night, and once again on high
the blazing sun forgets its course,

deep-hidden in that whirling smoke
from which the floods of Nile may fall.
But summer burns the city still.
The metal bird upon the wall
is silent; Shirley and her clerk

in tiled and fireproof corridors
touch and fall apart. No fires
consume the banked comptometers;
no flood has lipped the inlaid floors.

Child with a Dead Animal

The thing you saw set your eyes running tears
    faster than words could tell:
the creature changed to thing, kindness to dread,
the live shape chilled, forsaken, left for dead —
    these crowded up to blind your eyes; these fell

and fell till it seemed you'd wash away with tears
    the glimpse you'd had of death
and clear it from your heart. It was not true.
The sight you saw had found its home in you;
    it breathes now in your breath,

sits in your glance. From it those gasping tears
    fell, and will always fall.
They sign you Man, whose very flesh is made
of light's encounter with its answering shade.
    Take then this bread, this wine; be part of all.

Naked Girl and Mirror

This is not I. I had no body once —
only what served my need to laugh and run
and stare at stars and tentatively dance
on the fringe of foam and wave and sand and sun.
Eyes loved, hands reached for me, but I was gone
on my own currents, quicksilver, thistledown.
Can I be trapped at last in that soft face?

I stare at you in fear, dark brimming eyes.
Why do you watch me with that immoderate plea —
"Look under these curled lashes, recognize
that you were always here; know me — be me."
Smooth once-hermaphrodite shoulders, too tenderly
your long slope runs, above those sudden shy
curves furred with light that spring below your space.

No, I have been betrayed. If I had known
that this girl waited between a year and a year,
I'd not have chosen her bough to dance upon.
Betrayed, by that little darkness here, and here
this swelling softness and that frightened stare
from eyes I will not answer; shut out here
from my own self, by its new body's grace —

for I am betrayed by someone lovely. Yes,
I see you are lovely, hateful naked girl.
Your lips in the mirror tremble as I refuse
to know or claim you. Let me go — let me be gone.
You are half of some other who may never come.
Why should I tend you? You are not my own;
you seek that other — he will be your home.

Yet I pity your eyes in the mirror, misted with tears;
I lean to your kiss. I must serve you; I will obey.
Some day we may love. I may miss your going, some day,
though I shall always resent your dumb and fruitful years.
Your lovers shall learn better, and bitterly too,
if their arrogance dares to think I am part of you.

Water

Water in braids and tumbles, shells of spray,
heaves of clear glass and solemn greeneyed pools,
eel-coils and quick meanders, goes its way
fretting this savage basalt with its tools,

where from the hot rock-edge I drop my hands
and see their bones spread out like tugging weed,
each finger double-winged with ampersands
that stand above the current's talking-speed.

Such sentences, such cadences of speech
the tonguing water stutters in its race

as may have set us talking each to each
before our language found its proper pace;

since we are channelled by its running stream.
A skin of water glitters on your eye,
and round your skull a halo of faint steam
breathes up to join the spindrift in the sky.

A Document

"Sign there." I signed, but still uneasily.
I sold the coachwood forest in my name.
Both had been given me; but all the same
remember that I signed uneasily.

Ceratopetalum, Scented Satinwood:
a tree attaining seventy feet in height.
Those pale-red calyces like sunset light
burned in my mind. A flesh-pink pliant wood

used in coachbuilding. Difficult of access
(those slopes were steep). But it was World War Two.
Their wood went into bomber-planes. They grew
hundreds of years to meet those hurried axes.

Under our socio-legal dispensation
both name and woodland had been given me.
I was much younger then than any tree
matured for timber. But to help the nation

I signed the document. The stand was pure
(eight hundred trees perhaps). Uneasily
(the bark smells sweetly when you wound the tree)
I set upon this land my signature.

Camping at Split Rock

Red mounting scales of cliff lead the eye up;
but here the rock has spaces of tenderness
where light and water open its heart. A lip
of narrow green shows where the creek-banks bless
a niche for trees and birds. So many birds!
Outside our tent they cross and recross our patch
of vision, hatch the air and double-hatch
in diving curves and lines. Each curve has words;

each flight speaks its own bird. The slowly strong
deep-thrusting heron's stroke; the glittering
daring rush of the swallow and the long
poise and turn of hawk on a still wing;
the quick low scuttle of wren, the coloured wind
of finches, blue-jay's wide noble rise and fall —
we read each bird from its air-written scrawl,
the bird no stranger than the interpreting mind.

The finger of age-old water splits the rock
and makes us room to live; the age-old word
runs on in language and from obstinate dark
hollows us room for seeing. The birds go by;
but we can name and hold them, each a word
that crystals round a more than mortal bird.

Snakeskin on a Gate

Summer's long heats slowing at January's end
I found by the gate a snake-slough; its dry scales
of horn blew newly-cast in the hot wind
against the hedge, ripped between stem and thorn.
I took it, shivering, and hung it on the gate-rails —

thinking it emblem, if emblems had been needed,
of a time of life like January, double-faced month of change,
that looking backward sighs for the dedication's innocence,
then turns too many pages, to find the end of the book.
But its touch was closer than omens: dry, cold, strange.

Dry with life withdrawn; cold with a desert cold;
strange, between two realities, neither alive nor decayed,
the snakeskin blew in the wind on the closed gate;
and I went uneasily, watching, for my life's sake,
for a coil of poisonous dark in the pools of shade.

Then at last I saw him, stretching warm in the sun;
shining; his patterned length clean as a cut jewel.
Set free of its dim shell, his glinting eye
saw only movement and light and had no fear of me.
Like this from our change, my soul, let us drink renewal.

Portrait

It was a heartfelt game, when it began —
polish and cook and sew and mend, contrive,
move between sink and stove, keep flower-beds weeded —
all her love needed was that it was needed,
and merely living kept the blood alive.

Now an old habit leads from sink to stove,
mends and keeps clean the house that looks like home,
and waits in hunger dressed to look like love
for the calm return of those who, when they come,
remind her: this was a game, when it began.

Turning Fifty

Having known war and peace
and loss and finding,
I drink my coffee and wait
for the sun to rise.

With kitchen swept, cat fed,
the day still quiet,
I taste my fifty years
here in the cup.

Outside the green birds come
for bread and water.
Their wings wait for the sun
to show their colours.

I'll show my colours too.
Though we've polluted
even this air I breathe
and spoiled green earth;

though, granted life or death,
death's what we're choosing,
and though these years we live
scar flesh and mind,

still, as the sun comes up
bearing my birthday,
having met time and love
I raise my cup —

dark, bitter, neutral, clean,
sober as morning —
to all I've seen and known —
to this new sun.

Shadow

(1970)

For One Dying

Come now; the angel leads.
All human lives betray,
all human love erodes
under time's laser ray;

the innocent animals
within us and without
die in corrupted hells
made out of human thought.

Green places and pure springs
are poisoned and laid bare —
even the hawk's high wings
ride on a fatal air.

But come; the angel calls.
Deep in the dreamer's cave
the one pure source upwells
its single luminous wave;

and there, Recorder, Seer,
you wait within your cell.
I bring, in love and fear,
the world I know too well

into your hands. Receive
these fractured days I yield.
Renew the life we grieve
by day to know and hold.

Renew the central dream
in blazing purity,
and let my rags confirm
and robe eternity.

For still the angel leads.
Ruined yet pure we go
with all our days and deeds
into that flame, that snow.

This Time Alone

Here still, the mountain that we climbed
when hand in hand my love and I
first looked through one another's eyes
and found the world that does not die.

Wild fuchsia flowered white and red,
the mintbush opened to the bee.
Stars circled round us where we lay
and dawn came naked from the sea.

Its holy ordinary light
welled up and blessed us and was blessed.
Nothing more simple, nor more strange,
than earth itself was then our rest.

I face the steep unyielding rock,
I bleed against the cockspur's thorn,
struggling the upward path again,
this time alone. This time alone,

I turn and set that world alight.
Unfurling from its hidden bud
it widens round me, past my sight,
filled with my breath, fed with my blood;

the sun that rises as I stand
comes up within me gold and young;
my hand is sheltered in your hand,
the bread of silence on my tongue.

Advice to a Young Poet

There's a carefully neutral tone
you must obey;
there are certain things you must learn
never to say.

The city may totter around you,
the girders split;
but don't take a prophetic stance,
you'll be sorry for it.

The stars may disappear
in a poisonous cloud,
you may find your breath choked out.
Please, not so loud.

Your fingers and hands have turned
into hooks of steel?
Your mind's gone electronic
and your heart can't feel?

But listen, your teachers tell you,
it's not to worry.
Don't stamp or scream; take the Exit door
if you must; no hurry.

No panic, and no heroics,
the market's steady.
No rocking the boat, we beg.

What — sunk already?

Weapon

The will to power destroys the power to will.
The weapon made, we cannot help but use it;
it drags us with its own momentum still.

The power to kill compounds the need to kill.
Grown out of hand, the heart cannot refuse it;
the will to power undoes the power to will.

Though as we strike we cry "I did not choose it,"
it drags us with its own momentum still.
In the one stroke we win the world and lose it.
The will to power destroys the power to will.

Stillborn

Those who have once admitted
within their pulse and blood
the chill of that most loving
that most despairing child
know what is never told —
the arctic anti-god,
the secret of the cold.

Those who have once expected
the pains of that dark birth
which takes but without giving

and ends in double loss —
they still reach hands across
to grave from flowering earth,
to shroud from living dress.

Alive, they should be dead
who cheated their own death,
and I have heard them cry
when all else was lying still
"O that I stand above
while you lie down beneath!"
Such women weep for love
of one who drew no breath
and in the night they lie
giving the breast to death.

Wings

Between great coloured vanes the butterflies
drift to the sea with fixed bewildered eyes.

Once all their world was food; then sleep took over,
dressed them in cloaks and furs for some great lover —

some Juan, some Helen. Lifted by air and dream
they rose and circled into heaven's slipstream

to seek each other over fields of blue.
Impassioned unions waited — can't-come-true

images. Blown, a message or a kiss,
earth sent them to the sun's tremendous Yes.

Once met and joined, they sank; complete and brief
their sign was fastened back upon the leaf;

empty of future now, the wind turned cold,
their rich furs worn, they thin to membraned gold.

Poor Rimbauds never able to return
out of the searing rainbows they put on,

their wings have trapped them. Staring helplessly
they blow beyond the headland, to the sea.

Letter

How write an honest letter
to you, my dearest?
We know each other well —
not well enough.

You, the dark baby hung
in a nurse's arms,
seen through a mist — your eyes
still vague, a stranger's eyes;

hung in a hospital world
of drugs and fevers.
You, too much wanted,
reared in betraying love.

Yes, love is dangerous.
The innocent beginner
can take for crystal-true
that rainbow surface;

surprise, surprise —
paddling the slime-dark bottom
the bull-rout's sting and spine
stuns your soft foot.

Why try to give
what never can be given —
safety, a green world?
It's mined, the trip-wire's waiting.

Perhaps we should have trained you
in using weapons,
bequeathed you a straight eye,
a sure-shot trigger-finger,

or that most commonplace
of self-defences,
an eye to Number One,
shop-lifting skills,

a fibrous heart, a head
sharp with arithmetic
to figure out the chances?
You'd not have that on.

What then? Drop-out, dry-rot?
Wipe all the questions
into an easy haze,
a fix for everything?

Or split the mind apart —
an old solution —
shouting to mental-nurses
your coded secrets?

I promised you unborn
something better than that —
the chance of love; clarity,
charity, caritas — dearest,

don't throw it in. Keep searching.
Dance even among these
poisoned swords; frightened only
of not being what you are —

of not expecting love
or hoping truth;
of sitting in lost corners
ill-willing time.

I promised what's not given,
and should repent of that,
but do not. You are you,
finding your own way;

nothing to do with me,
though all I care for.
I blow a kiss on paper.
I send your letter.

The Flame-Tree Blooms

It was you planted it;
and it grew high and put on crops of leaves,
extravagant fans; sheltered in it the spider weaves
and birds move through it.

For all it grew so well
it never bloomed, though we watched patiently,
having chosen its place where we could see
it from our window-sill.

Now, in its eighteenth spring,
suddenly, wholly, ceremoniously
it puts off every leaf and stands up nakedly,
calling and gathering

every capacity in it, every power,
drawing up from the very roots of being
this pulse of total red that shocks my seeing
into an agony of flower.

It was you planted it;
and I lean on the sill to see it stand
in its dry shuffle of leaves, just as we planned,
these past years feeding it.

Australia 1970

Die, wild country, like the eaglehawk,
dangerous till the last breath's gone,
clawing and striking. Die
cursing your captor through a raging eye.

Die like the tigersnake
that hisses such pure hatred from its pain
as fills the killer's dreams
with fear like suicide's invading stain.

Suffer, wild country, like the ironwood
that gaps the dozer-blade.
I see your living soil ebb with the tree
to naked poverty.

Die like the soldier-ant
mindless and faithful to your million years.
Though we corrupt you with our torturing mind,
stay obstinate; stay blind.

For we are conquerors and self-poisoners
more than scorpion or snake
and dying of the venoms that we make
even while you die of us.

I praise the scoring drought, the flying dust,
the drying creek, the furious animal,
that they oppose us still;
that we are ruined by the thing we kill.

Communication

My three-day friend met on the edge of dying,
I write these lines for you,
your line, they tell me, being disconnected.
I send this message though it won't get through.

Three days and nights we talked out to each other
our separate pains, deeper than strangers do.
Your number's disconnected now for ever,
but I talk on, though not to you.

Die as we must, we two were then related
in human honesty and suffering.
Only the buzz of silence meets me now,
I dial, but there's no one answering.

Yet I must go on talking to you dying.
I need to argue how we're held together,
how a connection brings a line alive
since we are all connected with each other.

"The heart is one" (sang Baez); it can get through.
Through the impersonal gabble of exchanges
lights suddenly flash on, the circuit pulses,
joins us together briefly, then estranges.

The line goes dead, but still the line is there,
for our reality is in relation.
The current bears the message, then stops flowing;
but it has proved there is communication.

The Unnecessary Angel

Yes, we still can sing
who reach this barren shore.
But no note will sound
as it did before.

In selfless innocence
first the song began.
Then it rose and swelled
into the song of man.

Every tone and key,
every shade it learned
that its limits held
and its powers discerned:

love and history,
joy in earth and sun,
its small chords embraced,
joining all in one.

But no note can come
from the flesh's pride
once the weapon's lodged
in the bleeding side;

once the truth is known:
Law surpasses Art.
Not the heart directs
what happens to the heart.

Yet we still can sing,
this proviso made:
Do not take for truth
any word we said.

Let the song be bare
that was richly dressed.
Sing with one reserve:
Silence might be best.

Shadow

I stood to watch the sun
slip over the world's edge
its white-hot temples burning
where earth and vapour merge.
The shadow at my feet
rose upward silently;
announced that it was I;
entered to master me.

Yes, we exchange our dreams.
Possessed by day, intent
with haste and hammering time,
earth and her creatures went
imprisoned, separate
in isolating light.
Our enemy, our shadow,
is joined to us by night.

Joined by negating night
that counterpoints the day
and deepens into fear
of time that falls away,
of self that vanishes
till eyes stare outward blind
on one invading darkness
that brims from earth to mind.

Then came the after-image
burning behind the eye,
single and perilous

but more than memory.
When universe is lost
man on that centre stares
where from the abyss of power
world's image grows and flares.

World's image grows, and chaos
is mastered and lies still
in the resolving sentence
that's spoken once for all.
Now I accept you, shadow,
I change you; we are one.
I must enclose a darkness
since I contain the Sun.

Alive: Poems 1971–1972

(1973)

From *Habitat*

IX

We were fortunate, house; in a world of exiles
stateless, homeless, wandering, spying, murdering,
wars, bewilderments, losses and betrayals,
we found each other.
In your spaces and awkward corners
we spread our lives out, fitted and grew together.

Your old trees dying warmed us with winter fires.
Your birdcalls, mice in cupboards, snakes in the garden,
made welcomes and nuisances for us, panics and symbols.
We ceased to be strangers.
Oiling your creaking hinges,
cursing your ill-hung doors, we changed in mute exchanges.

Storms beat in from the west, from eastward cyclones.
The traffic outside, the wars and rumours of wars,
the sad lost voices, the glow and rumble of cities,
you muted for us.
The radio plugged in your wiring,
let in, when we chose, enough of that surge and chorus.

Inside the books were read and the words were scribbled,
the talk went on, the friends and enemies came

and went; but we were content, coherent, employed
on our true affairs.
Our sicknesses, love and quarrels
continued in and around your beds and chairs.

What came in from outside was absorbed or wasted.
A pouring current of things and words and food
came channelled through doors and telephone, comings and
    goings.
People attract and direct
that current, are its transformers,
stations in space and time. We choose or reject

what passes us on the streams that circle the world.
Some things enter and leave, some become at home,
some are unanswered, irrelevant, turned away.
A kind of weaving
goes on all the time in houses, its pattern
determined by the years of taking and giving.

And we were fortunate, house, to have your shelter.
Your roof crouched among trees on the turning planet,
part of a surface receiving rain and sunlight,
kept off the shrieking
speed of space, the bad weather,
enclosed our portion of time, our pattern of making.

Thanks for our luck; against all accusations
from the forlorn, the victims whirled in the wind,
I look back over our time here and affirm it,
having that right.
To live, to work together in intimate peace
is to prove in the dark the quality of light.

From *Some Words*

UNLESS

132   Had a whole dream once
          full of nothing else.

A bottomless pit,
eyes bulged out
across it,
neck stretched
over it.

A whole life I know of
fell into it
once;
and never came back.

NEVER

Should never have done it, never.
Should never have left that country
where I was queen entirely.
Treacherous thaws betrayed me.

That land of I-will-never
gleaming with snow and silence
suited me with its iceblink,
its blue eyes fixed as mirrors.

Set on my peak, I queened it.
It was the spring that took me,
drowning in warmer waters
out to the lands of sometimes.

Here in the lands of sometimes
I stretched out hands lamenting,
but I'm a queen no longer,
melted my snows and glaciers.

They were so strong, so solid,
crystal as tears long frozen.
Here I'm at risk, half-drowning,
wanting my season, winter.

It will return and find me
caught in a depth of water,
freezing unseen in ice-depths,
never again to queen it,

to sit on my peak unmoving
the sceptre cold in my fingers,
my eyes on the blue-eyed glacier.
Should never have left it, never.

FOREVER

Ah, but I had to leave it.
No one can live there always,
the frost-bound queen of Never.
Once the blood moves, the flood moves,

the thaw begins, the ice-peaks
crumble, dissolve to river,
in which I swim or founder
through the warm lands of sometimes;

swim, drown, but now am human.
Change is my true condition,
to take and give and promise,
to fight and fail and alter.

I aim towards Forever,
but that is no one's country,
till in perhaps one moment,
dying, I'll recognise it;

those peaks not ice but sunlit
from sources past my knowing,
its beauty of completion
the end of being human.

Dialogue

All dialogue's a bargain:
while A supplies the words
B adds the silence.
Or here's the poem

set on a blank of paper.
The music's pattern
is eloquent only against its intervals.

So, sometimes,
half-lost in thought or reading,
I raise unfocussed eyes.
Some luck of shadow
sets you in your own chair —
seen, not by will imagined,
simply because I need your silence there.

I half-start up, half-speak;
even that half is made out of my knowledge
that you are gone. It comes
not from the time we spent together
but from the years without you:
the film's dark negative,
the silence after talk.

Your not-being's true
just as your being was.
It circles me, a lightless moon
seen by my light.
The years of unrelation
complete you for me.

All that I see says blandly,
"I'm Now, I'm three-dimensional";
yes, but what else?
Concave backs convex.
Turn Presence inside out

Absence is demonstrated.
Flick off the conscious switch,
there's Nothing, sprung
out of its secret place behind the world.

So here's our dialogue
made out of plus and minus,
zero and number.

I play with world's this-side —
but did we ever find that smooth magician
much more than half-convincing?

Space Between

Space between lip and lip
and space between
living and long-dead flesh
can sometimes seem the same.

We strive across, we strain
to those who breathe the air,
to those in memory;
but Here is never There.

What is the space between,
enclosing us in one
united person, yet
dividing each alone?

Frail bridges cross from eye
to eye, from flesh to flesh,
from word to word; the net
is gapped at every mesh,

and this each human knows:
however close our touch
or intimate our speech,
silences, spaces reach
most deep, and will not close.

Lament for Passenger Pigeons

Don't ask for the meaning, ask for the use.
                              — Wittgenstein

The voice of water as it flows and falls
the noise air makes against earth-surfaces
have changed; are changing to the tunes we choose.

What wooed and echoed in the pigeon's voice?
We have not heard the bird. How reinvent
that passenger, its million wings and hues,

when we have lost the bird, the thing itself,
the sheen of life on flashing long migrations?
Might human musics hold it, could we hear?

Trapped in the fouling nests of time and space,
we turn the music on; but it is man,
and it is man who leans a deafening ear.

And it is man we eat and man we drink
and man who thickens round us like a stain.
Ice at the polar axis smells of me.

A word, a class, a formula, a use:
that is the rhythm, the cycle we impose.
The sirens sang us to the ends of sea,

and changed to us; their voices were our own,
jug-jug to dirty ears in dirtied brine.
Pigeons and angels sang us to the sky

and turned to metal and a dirty need.
The height of sky, the depth of sea we are,
sick with a yellow stain, a fouling dye.

Whatever Being is, that formula,
it dies as we pursue it past the word.
We have not asked the meaning, but the use.

What is the use of water when it dims?
The use of air that whines an emptiness?
The use of glass-eyed pigeons caged in glass?

We listen to the sea, that old machine,
to air that hoarsens on earth-surfaces
and has no angel, no migrating cry.

What is the being and the end of man?
Blank surfaces reverb a human voice
whose echo tells us that we choose to die:

or else, against the blank of everything,
to reinvent that passenger, that bird-
siren-and-angel image we contain
essential in a constellating word.
To sing of Being, its escaping wing,
to utter absence in a human chord
and recreate the meaning as we sing.

Alive

Light; and water. One drop.
Under the microscope
an outline. Slight
as a rim of glass;
barely and sparely there,
a scarcely-occupied shape.

What's more, the thing's alive.
How do I recognise
in a fleck so small

no human term applies —
no word's so minimal —
life's squirming throb and wave?

Locked in the focussed stare
of the lens, my sight
flinches: a tiny kick.
The life in me replies
signalling back
"You there: I here."
What matters isn't size.

What matters is . . . form. Form
concentrated, exact,
proof of a theorem
whose lines are lines of force
marking a limit. Trim,
somehow matter-of-fact,
even matter-of-course.
But alive. Like my eyes. Alive.

To Mary Gilmore

Having arranged for the mail and stopped the papers,
tied loaves of bread Orlando-like to the tree,
love-messages for birds; suitcase in hand
I pause and regard the irony of me.

Supposed to be fifty-six, hair certainly grey,
stepping out much like sixteen on another journey
through a very late spring, the conference-papers packed
as a half-excuse for a double-tongued holiday;

as though I believed — well, then, as though I believed.
Remember Mary Gilmore, her little son
turned sixty-four, and bald? And Mary playing
her poet's game as though she'd never be done.

This is my place. It isn't far to my grave,
the waiting stone. But still there's life to do
and a taste of spring in the air. Should I sit and grieve,
Mary, or keep the ink running, like you?

Years have their truths, and each as true as another.
Salute, Mary. Not long now till we know
the blackened deathly world you once foresaw;
but now — let's live. I pick up my case and go.

"Bid Me Strike a Match and Blow"

Set the match. Watch how the fire begins.
A wince, a flicker, blue,
the full gold at the core.
Spreading, it grips like teeth,
draws air like breath.
It has a work to do,
centuries of deadwood for raging through.
That's how the fire begins.

Air is its object and it thrives on air.
All that is burnable
waits for its change, inert.
Fuel and air commune within the fire,
a vanishing, a trance,
a final dance
alters their being. Stare
into its upward hastening for
some sign of visible God.
For nothing is more pure than fire in air.

Trees rise in it; whole dying forests rise,
whole peoples made of flame
storm upwards and are gone:
flights of death-ridden birds,

the fur and fear of blazing animals.
Earth's sap and emerald
die in a central gold;
drawn tall to dervishes of smoke they rise.

The speech of fire is all an upward prayer,
evangel to convert
to primal purity
all pasts that die,
all time's long error and black history
to be a speck of carbon in the sky.

Tableau

Bent over, staggering in panic or despair
from post to parking-meter in the hurried street,
he seemed to gesture at me,
as though we had met again; had met somewhere
forgotten, and now for the last time had to meet.

And I debated with myself; ought I to go
over the road — since no one stopped to ask
or even stand and look —
abandon my own life awhile and show
I was too proud to shirk that ant-like task?

And finally went. His almost vanished voice
accepted me; he gave himself to my hold,
(*pain, cancer — keep me still*).
We leaned on a drinking-fountain, fused in the vice
of a double pain; his sweat dropped on me cold.

Holding him up as he asked till the ambulance came,
among the sudden curious crowd, I knew
his plunging animal heart,
against my flesh the shapes of his too-young bone,
the heaving pattern of ribs. As still I do.

Warding the questioners, bearing his rack of weight,
I drank our strange ten minutes of embrace,
and watched him whiten there,
the drenched poverty of his slender face.
We could have been desperate lovers met too late.

Picture

So eagerly lightly the man
stroked his colours on —
the tawny sleepy slopes
the mood-dark mountains behind
and the fall and change of light
through clouds gentler than blue.
I stroke his hills too,
their bodies stretched in the mind.

Can only the young love
like this, with so tender a hand
and eye, see so
purely the earth's moment?
Past middle-age, I fidget,
pick at the years' callus
that cataracts my sight,
dulls my hand like a glove.

In what he paints I see
an earth I used to know,
light stroking slopes aglow,
earth various as flesh
and flesh its own delight;
and feel the young man stroking
his love, his earth, with a hand.
Time locks us up in the mind,
but leaves this window, art.

Grace

Living is dailiness, a simple bread
that's worth the eating. But I have known a wine,
a drunkenness that can't be spoken or sung
without betraying it. Far past Yours or Mine,
even past Ours, it has nothing at all to say;
it slants a sudden laser through common day.

It seems to have nothing to do with things at all,
requires another element or dimension.
Not contemplation brings it; it merely happens,
past expectation and beyond intention;
takes over the depth of flesh, the inward eye,
is there, then vanishes. Does not live or die,

because it occurs beyond the here and now,
positives, negatives, what we hope and are.
Not even being in love, or making love,
brings it. It plunges a sword from a dark star.

Maybe there was once a word for it. Call it grace.
I have seen it, once or twice, through a human face.

That Seed

That seed I took from a low branch
of a rain-forest tree
wore a red fruit like an apple
that might have poisoned me;

but I set and watered it,
waited day by day.
Nothing seemed to come of it.
I threw the soil away.

143

Now in the garden where it fell,
quite against my plan,
springs up a thing as stray, as fierce,
as tall as a grown man.

Should I take an axe to it?
Should I let it grow?
It will shade my window-sill
and choke the flowers below.

It will beat its wild arms
in winds against my wall.
It may smash my roof down
if storm should make it fall.

Damn the unexpected!
I don't know.
Shall I take an axe to it
or shall I let it grow?

Black/White

This time I shall recover
from my brief blowtorch fever.
The sweats of living
flood me; I wake again,
pondering the moves of anti and of pro.
Back into play I go.

Had it been pro-biotics that they gave me
would I still live?
Anti-biotics maybe snub the truth,
cheating the black king's move —
emptily save me,
a counter-ghost tricked from a rightful death.

But you can play on black squares or on white,
do without counters even; in theory
even the dead still influence what we do,
direct our strategy.
I'm none too sure exactly why I'm here,
which side I'm playing for —

But still, here's day, here's night,
the checkerboard of yes and no
and take and give.
Again I meet you face to face,
which in itself is unexpected grace.
To arms, my waiting opposite —
we live.

Fourth Quarter

(1976)

Fourth Quarter

You bitter sign,
last lemon-quarter grin,
tell me to throw it in?
I won't resign.

Tomorrow you'll be gone
into the black;
but you're just moving on
to make your comeback.

I won't be back again
or not this way.
But still there's gold to win
from the mullock's clay.

Old, terribly old
to the scornful young,
but still this rim of gold,
this last-light tongue

touches me till I shiver.
Grin in the sky,
I'm taker still and giver:
there's your reply.

Easter Moon and Owl

Keeping your old appointment,
spring's northern dawn,
you bring in autumn here.
The god's long done for in this hemisphere;
your full-tide flood of light
won't set him rising.

But the same owl, your ancient messenger,
crosses that light, his call
sounds here as there. Ruler of women
and singler-out of poets,
I greet him as your servant.

Men spy you out with eyes.
Their red brand's on your flank
and they plan colonies.
As for us, your true citizens,
we'll never make it
into those well-controlled
and solar-heated settlements.

Yet we still drag his tides.
His salt blood's subject
to the old spells of women
as to your own, Selene.
He fears the night, and still our music draws him.

To you, chill Domina,
I make the prayer of age. In my last quarter
let me be hag, but poet.
The lyric note may vanish from my verse,
but you have also found acceptable
the witch's spell —
even the witch's curse.

Muse, if they mock you,
you may yet grin last.
Man's signs are ominous.

Tightropes

Lacking in one capacity, you need another,
fair balance at the end of the pole,
to walk the tightropes. Some people
are unable to see horizons, but compensate
by concentrating intensely
on the next two steps ahead.

I've cultivated stability
by keeping my horizons straight.
Now of a sudden we're crossing
very mountainous country. The peaks around
draw my attention to the gulfs below;
I'm suffering from nausea. Dangerous for acrobats,
this upness and downness, the landscape running crazy.

Concentrate, woman, concentrate.
Free verse is harder to bring off than rhyme,
liberty than slavery. Remember,
the pole-end weight, the accepted convention,
has dropped off.
Nor are you equipped with an inbuilt spirit-level.

Late in life, though, to acquire the habit
long unadmired in others
of seeing no further than the pace or two ahead
on a quaking rope.

Interface (III)

Whales die of a sort of madness:
They choose their own beaching.
Watch them come in like liners

under deranged captains.

Try to turn such whales aside
back to deep waters —
obstinately, blindly, certainly
they'll find another beach.

Death is inside the whale,
some diseased directive,
some inner treachery,
some worm lodged in the brain.

Afterwards, the whole air
of the coast's tainted
with an enormity,
corruption's total takeover.

You cannot bury the whale
in the beach it chose.
No sand is deep enough.
Some king-tide will uncover it.

Men must come, wearing masks
against decay's contagion,
chop it into small portions,
bulldoze it into trucks,

Far off, please. Very far off
where the smell of death can't reach us.
It's a huge task
to do away with a whale.

Whales are great mammals
but no wiser than men.
Take the head, you scientists,
investigate its workings.

You may find, deep in there,
the secret of destruction,
the tiny burrowing worm,
the virus in the brain.

You may expound its reason,
but the whale's past cure.
It has finally rejected
the whale-road, the free seas.

If you mourn its choice, remember,
not only whales have made it.
Whole peoples, countries, nations
have died in the same way.
Galaxies may be strewn
with staring burnt-out planets
which took that path.

But this is to mourn a whale —
only a whale.

Dream

A degree or two of fever, a dose of aspirin,
and somewhere past midnight,
I think I wake from a dream.

So banal it was wholly convincing;
the clothes authentic, the set
three-dimensional, the cast and direction
faultless. The howling green hills of sea
storming the island and estuary
were quite familiar, attacking a country
whose map was clear in my mind. I remembered
everything as though I had lived there, though
I had never lived there.

A boring plot enough. First the Escape,
the door unlocked at dawn, the two,
trembling from hunger and torture,
waiting for the rescue-boat.

Then the Pursuit, the Capture, the Betrayal,
the roll of friends in the enemy's hands;
the Disaster; this time final. Nothing retrieved,
the known world lost, diced away
among the inhuman powers.

I had been so entirely convinced.
Waking was such a relief. I almost heard
the parent soothing: it's all right darling,
you are perfectly safe. This is the real world
and look, nobody's dying, nobody's being tortured,
the world is safe as houses.
Go back to sleep.

Obediently,
I lie back repeating
"No one is dying, nobody's being tortured,
this is the real world and perfectly safe."

Eve Sings

These human words, this apple-song,
I take from our green world that dies.
I give them into your human hands,
I look into your human eyes.

Can it be we who grow so old
or is it the world? Poor world —
the worms in your apple foul and waste
the apple and the apple-taste.

Your second-Eden promises
fail like the first, though still we love.
Strain for one more essential kiss —
such greed and joy it's been to live
to the end of earth and all it was.

The knowledge was of evil and good.
We learn it deeper, growing old,
but cannot change our human mould
or nay the word the serpent said.

The apple's bitter to the mouth,
our last windfall from green earth.
The sword turns all ways and the tree
drops one last fruit for you and me.
I gather it for your human hands
I look into your human eyes.

Eve Scolds

Still so entrepreneurial, vulgarly moreish,
plunging on and exploring where there's nothing
left to explore, exhausting the last of our flesh.
Poor Natura; poor Eve.
Sungods are parvenu. I never could believe
that old rib-story you told.
You, to come first? It was Night, Water,
Earth, Love, I.
You Adam, son of the Sun —
you thought his maleness chose
you out of the unshaped clay
(his huge masculine beard, his dictator-hand
giving you strength). But I —
I *was* the clay. Little boys
have to invent such tales.
It's insecurity — always your trouble. You say
I nag you, hag of the night
drawing attention to your weaknesses.

But my trouble was love —
wanting to share my apples. You
called that temptation, put us both in with Him.
Not fair; I should have run home to Mother.

Now, it's too late. I could never decide to leave.
Wholly bewizarded,
bullied, used as you use us, I rather liked it —
asked for it, no doubt.
But you and I, at heart, never got on.
Each of us wants to own —
you, to own me, but even more, the world;
I, to own you.

Lover, we've made, between us,
one hell of a world. And yet —
still at your touch I melt. How can there be
any way out of this?
As always, I go overboard for you,
here at the world's last edge.
Ravage us still; the very last green's our kiss.

The Eucalypt and the National Character

(for Sir Otto Frankel)

*I believe it is the casual informality of form, so much in keeping with
what one has come to regard as the national character, which has given
the eucalypts their unrivalled place in the Australian landscape, and in our
perception and consciousness of Australia.*

— O. H. Frankel, UNESCO Symposium on
Man and Landscape, Canberra 1974

Yes, we do perceive her as sprawling and informal;
even dishevelled, disorderly. That may be because
we are still of two minds about militarism and class-systems.
When we are informal, we're half-afraid of bad form.
She, on the other hand, follows a delicate bent
of her own. Worn by such aeons, dried by such winds,
she has learned to be flexible, spare, flesh close to the bone.   *153*

Ready for any catastrophe, every extreme,
she leaves herself plenty of margin. Nothing is stiff,
symmetrical, indispensable. Everything bends
whip-supple, pivoting, loose, with a minimal mass.
She can wait grimly for months to break into flower
or willingly bloom in a day when the weather is right.
Meagre, careless, indifferent? With the toughest care,
the most economical tenderness, she provides for seed and egg.

Nor is she ever vulgar; she commits no excesses.
Her various gestures surround our pine plantations,
those fat green regiments that gobble our noble hills,
letting no light through, bearing no flowers. She is all light,
breathes in the noonday as lovers their lovers' breath.
We darken her sky with our cities.
She is artist enough to manage a graceful asymmetry·
but we are more apt to turn crooks.

Growing-Point

A child in early spring, I stared
up at the sapling's growing-point;
a gathered strength, a total thrust
muscling itself, its swirl and sheaf
to one high clench of folded leaf.

My body answered tiptoe there,
a central need to rise as high
as limit, balance, let you go.
Around that axis spreads the weight
tree can afford by growing straight.

Breadth, form, completion — those depend
upon a proper symmetry.
The length of branch, the stance in space,
what leaf and fruit tree can sustain
154   dispose around a central strain.

I knew no word for growing-point,
but in myself the sapling rose,
an aim, a need, a leap to air;
where weighted, rounded, bough on bough
the tree fills out its limits now.

Creation–Annihilation

God in his element
pleased with his work and play
under the firmament
started the fifth great day.
Building the Elephant
from new-created mud,
whizzed round by fins and wings,
fishy and birdy things,
"Good," shouted God.

Slow Hippopotami
heaved from his clayey hand.
The golden Lion's eye
took light at his command.
Happy Hyena's cry,
roar of the Crocodile
answered his hearty voice:
"After your kind, rejoice
and be my Animal."

Mudscraps and sparks of light
he scattered everywhere.
Motes from his hand's delight
crowded earth, water, air,
too small, it seemed, for care;
too small for Adam's eye
when all the names began.
None of the words of man
reached lower than the Fly.

Anton van Leeuwenhoek
(seventeenth century)
— he was the first to look
into that squirming sea
under the Holy Book.
Ova and sperm he saw
under his single lens
down where the world begins —
animalcule and spore.

Minute, despised, the Fleas
sprang to appalling size.
Knee-joints of ants and bees;
wing-scales of butterflies;
weevils in granaries;
unseen rotifera
perfect as Elephant
waved all their cilia —
("Mere scraps and huslement"
of the Creation, as
Adam had thought they were.)

Already shaken by
crazy Galileo
whose telescopic eye
had set earth spinning so,
no one in bed could lie
safe, with those skies below,
man saw each water-drop
crowded with life and death.
How could he draw a breath?
Where would the worries stop?

Motion was everywhere,
all rules were running wild.
Man called to God in fear,
"Once I was Favourite Child!
Now I feel insecure,
creatures infest my blood,

I take no step that's sure,
even my food's impure.
Where are you, father, God?"

God, who had graduated
as any artist should,
beyond what he'd created
once he had seen it good,
was nowhere to be found,
by any man-made lens.
"He's died. He's gone to ground.
Theology's unsound.
He's become simply Ens!"

He left us in his will
(an ancient testament)
the whole Creation. Still,
insulted and bereft,
belittled by the sky,
besieged by the unseen,
we wonder angrily
how he could be so mean.

"His job was all Creation.
What is there left to do
but turn our talent to
what's always been its bent?
That must be what he meant.
Our job's Annihilation!"

The Marks

Suddenly seeing my hand —
obedient bored pen-holder —
there on the field of paper,
I notice that oblong scar

at the base of the right forefinger.
That one's the first I remember.

A three-year-old, related
to me by memory only,
tripped and fell on a rock
(or was it a piece of glass?
I forget the agent enemy).
The world went scarlet with shock
and shook with appalling noise
like the yell of a branded calf.

Sting of rank iodine, scream
of linen ripped for a bandage,
and over the blood and grief
somebody's careless voice,
"The mark might stay till you die."

Die? Die? Die?
Like a fly or a sheep? A word
to strike you dumb on a sob.
If dying is what will happen
how shall I manage this trap
of a skin so ready to bleed,
and this hurtable bagful of red
in a world of sting and slap
and cut and knock and stab?

A long white line where the knife
slipped off a loaf of bread;
a nip from a blue mud-crab;
a scar from a barbed-wire jag;
a criss-cross pucker of burn;
a callus left by a pen;
a knuckle twisted by pain;
a random scribble of vein.

I have kept my skinful of red
on this hinged scaffold of bone
(with all due gratitude

to the help of medical science).
I have learned not to tumble down;
I can dodge and parry and hide;
I can handle kettle and knife.
It has been an enlightening life.

We have held off the enemy
and welcomed the friend and lover;
it has been a long alliance.
Director to employee
Hand: let's salute each other
though the mark of each failed encounter
will certainly stay till we die.

Cold Night

Rain at the windows; in the house
a settled night of tearlessness.
That night a man came to my door
whom I had scarcely seen before.

Rain on his face and his hair wet
he looked a refugee from night,
hasty and trembling. One hard kiss
and he fled out to his own house.

I washed that kiss out of my mouth
cold as the rain that he ran through.
I'd my own troubles to hold in.
I never saw that man again —

dead. Dying then, the neighbours said,
and nothing to me, living or dead;

but walking sometimes on cold nights
the showers strike my naked face
hard, sudden, in a kind of kiss.

Patterns

Too long away, too far,
now I come back to you;
the seven stones
the brown clay jar,
the carved seashell,
still in your former place,
familiar peace
persisting still.

You are confirmed again;
you link with the old pattern in my brain
and time rejoins.

My eyes ache. I've been halfway round the world,
telescoped days and stretched them out again.
New faces, voices, wants; ribbons of roads and air
wound in and then unwound,
drained
answers from blood, hand, mind.

Be my old silence. Be
the place and past and pattern that I know.
Be a loved verse re-read
before I pick my duties up and go.

Envy

Envy, the artist's inescapable sin,
takes no account of difference, distance, space,
time, tradition, medium, age or race.
I want to have been in every hand and skin,

held every painter's brush and writer's pen
and sculptor's chisel. What a greeneyed pain

caught me staring at tigers in the temple of Nanzen-
ji last year! They were my tigers, mine.

But most of all it's reading poetry
makes me storm my limits like a jaguar's cage.
My hair and fingers crisp with jealousy
wanting this poem and that in hopeless rage.

If we've a heaven or hell, art's daemon will announce
to my arriving soul in either one,
"You can be — you are — whatever you envied once.
What you longed to have done is waiting to be done

"and all the boundaries are taken away.
You are Dante, Emily Brontë or Beethoven,
you can build the Taj Mahal, be Li Po or Manet.
Ask for a power and it shall be given."

Holding all skill and tradition, all times and eyes,
feeling the chill of the poles of art, the blaze
of its equator where the moment of making lies,
all lives and visions our own; past nights and days

my raging kin, we'd shape eternity
into earth's image, make the unseen seen
in forms of immutable jade. What hell or heaven could be
our proper justice, envy's retribution
or the reward of hopeless long devotion,
but reaching the highest power of what we've been?

Counting in Sevens

Seven ones are seven.
I can't remember that year
or what presents I was given.

Seven twos are fourteen.
That year I found my mind,
swore not to be what I had been.

Seven threes are twenty-one.
I was sailing my own sea,
first in love, the knots undone.

Seven fours are twenty-eight;
three false starts had come and gone;
my true love came, and not too late.

Seven fives are thirty-five.
In her cot my daughter lay,
real, miraculous, alive.

Seven sixes are forty-two.
I packed her sandwiches for school,
I loved my love and time came true.

Seven sevens are forty-nine.
Fruit loaded down my apple-tree,
near fifty years of life were mine.

Seven eights are fifty-six.
My lips still cold from a last kiss,
my fire was ash and charcoal-sticks.

Seven nines are sixty-three, seven tens are seventy,
Who would that old woman be?
She will remember being me,
but what she is I cannot see.

Yet with every added seven,
some strange present I was given.

Boundaries

One leaf-scrap, photographed this way,
lies in a whole leaf-pattern — that's surprising?
the whole plant-history's coded in one seed
and not just plant: the whole planet, its changes,
its wobble and spin, air, water, stars,
the sun's force, the moon's pull, wax and wane.
You might find ways to photograph all that.
But there's no need.
I've seen even a hat
build under itself a person long since dead.
That lock of wild bronze hair
that Byron cut from a girl's head
sprang under my touch alive with the whole girl.

It's just that we think in limit, form and time.
Only language invents
future and past (now's gone before it's said).
What's I, what's here?
It's the whole flow that's real,
the whole change pouring through the lens of eyes
that first distinguish, then forget distinction;
record the many, then rejoin the all.

Unpacking Books

(for Derek Walcott)

On a dusty floor among piled rocking towers,
block-forts of prose, philosophy, history,
criticism, politics, sciences — word-cities
of civilization's greying geography —
I pick you up, poet of loves and pities,

and from green Caribbean nights again you sing,
This banjo-world have one string
and all men does dance to that tune.
Yes, yes and yes, my blood answers,
takes up the tune and dances.

You too know the greedy fever's aftermath,
legacies of dead empires, the bitter taste
of warring faction, the natal land's slow death,
all energy, fertility, fruit ripped out to waste.

The rot remains with us, the men are gone . . .
Whatever we sang, dead politics denied;
the ruined rivers died, the forests died.
Yet poets keep an oath to hold and praise
what lives beyond the power-dreams of England,
    America, Spain.
Sweet naked Anadyomene drifts in to shore again
through oil-slicks, plastic discards, in our days.

Traherne said nothing had been loved as much
as it deserves. Though growing old I lament
too few answers to beauty's sight and touch,
too many words, I sit here now intent
on poetry's ancient vow to celebrate lovelong
life's wholeness, spring's return, the flesh's tune.

I twang that string again, rehearse the song
all ages sing, the dance I still remember,
taking a rhythm, a cue, a note from you,
player of violin and marimba.
There's an essential music still, a moon
where no man's landed, drawer of the heart
and muse of all our passion and our art.

Index of Titles

DATE DUE

Demco, Inc. 38-293